American Association of Community and Junior Colleges
National Center for Higher Education
One Dupont Circle, NW, Suite 410
Washington, DC 20036-1176
(202) 728-0200

© Copyrighted 1991
Printed in the United States of America
ISBN 0-87117-237-2

ADVANCI

HUMANITII STUDIES

AT COMMUNITY, TECHNICAL, AND JUNIOR COLLEGES

■

BY

DIANE U. EISENBERG

JAMES F. GOLLATTSCHECK

DIANA H. METCALF

BARBARA C. SHAPIRO

THIS AACJC PUBLICATION WAS PREPARED WITH FUNDING FROM
NATIONAL ENDOWMENT FOR THE HUMANITIES

ii

CONTENTS

Part I
PREFACE
Dale Parnell

WITH THE PUBLICATION OF *ADVANCING Humanities Studies at Community, Technical, and Junior Colleges,* the American Association of Community and Junior Colleges (AACJC), supported by a grant from the National Endowment for the Humanities (NEH), has completed a two-year effort to advance humanities education on some sixty community college campuses. Through its description of this year's *Advancing the Humanities* project, this report offers interested faculty and administrators throughout the country the opportunity to learn about the ways in which a variety of community, technical, and junior colleges, each with its own set of needs, set about strengthening their humanities programs, and ultimately their whole institutions, through a range of activities affecting both curriculum and faculty development. Described within are case studies of eight exemplary humanities programs, updates on the activities of last year's twenty-four *Advancing the Humanities* colleges, and the highlights of this year's twenty-five *Advancing the Humanities* participants. Also included are selected resource materials.

Not content to rest on its laurels, AACJC is proud to announce that it has embarked on still another humanities initiative, described in Part VII of this publication. This time, with the cooperation of the Community College Humanities Association (CCHA) and funding from the National Endowment for the Humanities (NEH), AACJC is working toward strengthening humanities programs at fifty more community colleges across the country. Colleges selected to participate in the new initiative are attending regional conferences, receiving mentoring services, and assuming leadership roles in the creation of permanent regional humanities networks.

The American Association of Community and Junior Colleges congratulates participants in its humanities projects, both old and new. It looks back with pride to the series of previously conducted humanities activities that paved the way, such as the AACJC/NEH National Humanities Roundtable in 1985, an AACJC Board-approved Humanities Policy Statement in 1986, and its widely discussed monograph, *The Future of Humanities Education at Community, Technical, and Junior Colleges.* In addition, it looks forward with anticipation to continuing opportunities for maintaining its commitment to the importance of humanities study on community college campuses for many years to come.

Dale Parnell is president and chief executive officer of the American Association of Community and Junior Colleges.

Part II
FOREWORD
Judith Jeffrey Howard

I AM DELIGHTED TO EXTEND MY CONGRATU-lations to the American Association of Community and Junior Colleges, the project staff, the mentors, and the participating colleges for the fine work completed in the *Advancing the Humanities* project.  It is a continuing pleasure to share in their creativity, dedication, and enthusiasm for the work of providing students in two-year institutions with the very best possible humanities programs.

Everyone knows that students need much more than job training. They need the knowledge and insight, the versatility and discernment that will enable them to make informed decisions in their public and personal lives. All students can benefit from the breadth of experience to be gained in the study of literature and history, the range of perspectives in the study of philosophy, foreign languages, and cultures. Through the study of humanities, students enlarge their own experience and reach beyond that experience to increased understanding of themselves and the world beyond themselves. This project has made a significant contribution toward advancing this important work. I offer my compliments and best wishes to all participants as their work continues.

Judith Jeffrey Howard is program officer and coordinator for community colleges, National Endowment for the Humanities.

Part III
ABOUT THE *ADVANCING THE HUMANITIES* PROJECT

"Community college students should study the humanities for a seemingly simple reason—to gain knowledge and ability to think concretely about important social and personal questions and to communicate these thoughts through clear and effective written expression. The practical demands of life—both private and public—are illuminated and made more valuable by the study of the humanities."
—from AACJC Humanities Policy Statement

WITH THE PUBLICATION OF THIS REPORT, THE AMERICAN Association of Community and Junior Colleges (AACJC) celebrates the completion of the second consecutive year it has been awarded a grant by the National Endowment for the Humanities (NEH) to advance the role of the humanities in the nation's two-year colleges. The grant of $275,108 (representing eighty percent of total project costs) enabled AACJC to strengthen and expand its commitment to the humanities by continuing its *Advancing the Humanities* project. This past year, an additional twenty-five community colleges were selected to work with mentors from eight exemplary humanities programs already in operation. Three of the eight programs, all of which had been originally funded by NEH, were new to the project.

The continuation of the *Advancing the Humanities* project is also evidence that the reverberations generated by AACJC's 1985 Humanities Roundtable and its resulting Humanities Policies State-

5

ment are still being felt and responded to by community college administrators and faculty members across the country.

Once again, the goal of the project was to provide the selected community colleges with a comprehensive program of activities and services to aid them in implementing their individual humanities programs. Central to the project was the three-day National Humanities Conference attended by three-member teams from each college which consisted of two members of the college's humanities faculty and one administrator. The Conference was followed by a mentoring service which enabled mentors and teams to visit each others' colleges and communicate regularly by mail and telephone. *Advancing the Humanities News,* a networking service newsletter, was published periodically throughout the project period.

AACJC's National Humanities Conference

This year's National Humanities Conference was held at Airlie House in Airlie, Virginia, from March 29 through April 1, 1990. Participants attended plenary sessions, mentor/college-team workshops, and presentations of exemplary projects, and heard addresses at luncheons and dinners by Meyer Reinhold, a classics scholar from Boston University; Saul Sosnowski, chair, Spanish and Portuguese department, University of Maryland; and John F. Andrews, a Shakespearean scholar. At the opening plenary session they were welcomed by Dale Parnell, AACJC president, Judith Jeffrey Howard, NEH program officer, and George Vaughan, director, Center for Community College Education, George Mason University.

In her remarks, Howard noted that the *Advancing the Humanities* project is the latest in a long line of collaborations between NEH and AACJC. She told participants, "You were selected because you have a vision," and added, "At the end of these three days your vision will have been enhanced by new ideas and new colleagues."

Vaughan, a member of the project's selection committee, described the selection process to conference participants as "the most ethical process I've ever worked with . . . you are here because of the merit of your proposals." Twenty-five colleges were chosen to participate in this year's program from the fifty-eight colleges that applied. Other members of the selection committee were William Askins, executive director, Community College Humanities Association; Diane U.

Diana Metcalf, project coordinator, Judith Jeffrey Howard, NEH program officer, and Saul Sosnowski, chair, Department of Spanish and Portuguese, University of Maryland, at 1991 National Humanities Conference.

Eisenberg, AACJC project manager; Judith Jeffrey Howard; Landon C. Kirchner, assistant dean, Johnson County Community College, Overland Park, Kansas; Anne S. McNutt, president, Technical College of the Lowcountry, Beaufort, South Carolina; Jerry Sue Owens, president, Lakewood Community College, White Bear Lake, Minnesota; and James F. Gollattscheck (ex officio), project director and AACJC executive vice president.

"We are, first and foremost, institutions of higher learning," Vaughan asserted, "and the *Advancing the Humanities* project has much to do with ensuring that we remain so."

New to the National Humanities Conference this past year was a guidebook for mentors. Prepared by Landon C. Kirchner, project evaluator, with contributions by Judith Jeffrey Howard and the AACJC staff, the guidebook delineated the responsibilities of the mentors, beginning with preparations prior to the conference and including guidelines for making follow-up mentoring visits, hosting visits from their teams, and evaluation and reporting responsibilities. It was based on the experience of mentors and staff during the project's first year and responded to evaluations and comments of the college teams themselves. It focused on ways for both mentors and their teams to make the most of the three-day conference as well as on strategies for ensuring the feasibility of team action plans. In addition, new and experienced mentors met for an orientation program prior to the Conference and then daily during the Conference to learn from one another and to ensure that they were fulfilling their roles. As Landon Kirchner, who led these orientation sessions, reminded the mentors, "A really critical part of this project is what happens here at the National Humanities Conference."

The Conference was organized so that mentors and teams would have as much time as possible to meet with one another. Each team came to the Conference with a preliminary plan. During the course of the Conference, teams were given assignments by their mentors to aid them in focusing their attentions on key issues. Assignments ranged from brainstorming on what must take place at faculty meetings in order to produce a viable American literature program, to writing a course description, to listing specific course objectives. Said a member of one team, after two full days of conference activities, "We're taking shape here, and it's amazing how far we have come."

It was clear that each team brought with it a unique set of problems and possible solutions. Mentors responded to the needs of their teams with a broad range of strategies and techniques. Some offered concrete aid by sharing their own syllabi, others suggested making contact with still other mentors and conference participants who had had similar experiences and problems. One mentor reminded his team, "This is a conference about networking as much as anything." While one team appeared to have a stronger sense of what it didn't want than what it did want, another came to the Conference ready to select specific texts. Still another college team convinced its mentor that conference time would be more profitably spent in conferring with one another than in responding to a specific assignment.

Conference participants made the most of every free moment to meet informally, to share problems and solutions with other teams, to complete their assignments, and to organize their ideas for their final two-minute presentations. One team member stated, "For too long the humanities people at my community college have been stepchildren. . . this conference celebrates the important contribution we make, and I think that's vital."

Another ruefully admitted, "In our school we're afraid to try new things. But," he added, "the *Advancing the Humanities* project gave the administration the courage to try, and when our proposal was accepted, the administration felt it was a compliment to them. This will be the first interdisciplinary non-honors course we ever had at the College!"

Participants at the 1991 National Humanities Conference share a thoughtful moment during a break.

An important aspect of the three-day National Humanities Conference was the opportunity for participants to hear presentations by their mentors. Of special interest were descriptions of three new exemplary humanities programs: "Integrating the Humanities with Technical Careers," Kirkwood Community College, Cedar Rapids, Iowa, directed by Joseph Collins and Robert Sessions; "The Nature and Function of Greek Mythology," Prince George's Community College, Largo, Maryland, directed by Isa Engleberg; and "A Time to Think About Shakespeare," Nassau Community College, Garden City, New York, directed by Bernice Kliman. A detailed description of each of the three programs may be found in Part IV of this publication.

Drawing upon these three new programs as well as five exemplary programs from the project's first year, the twenty-five new *Advancing the Humanities* college teams, with the aid of their mentors, were able to formulate and to present an exciting array of action plans before the three-day National Humanities Conference was adjourned. Responding to the needs of their individual constituencies, many of the colleges focused on ways to integrate the humanities into career programs or to add an international dimension to existing humanities programs. Said mentor Evelyn Edson, "Both my teams did very productive work. I enjoyed working with them and feel that they will be able to follow through. I think this is in part a tribute to how the Conference was organized. It really encourages serious thinking and working."

In her evaluation of the Conference, mentor Isa Engleberg asserted: "For both my teams, initial caution soon disappeared and my problem became one of containment rather than encouragement. The 'fallout' from the Conference will be considerable. It may not result precisely in the action plans described at the concluding session, but it will result in advancement for the humanities at each and every participating community college."

Participants felt the effects of their conference experience long after the meeting was adjourned. Dean Sandra Kurtinitis wrote to AACJC: "I just wanted to let you know how wonderful the National Humanities Conference was for those of us from Berkshire Community College who were lucky enough to attend . . . most exciting for me was to watch the epiphany of my faculty as they realized that NEH funds were available to help revitalize them and their colleagues as teachers and as scholars of the humanities. In short, if you were to measure the success of the weekend by the impact it has had on a small college in western Massachusetts, you can count your conference highly successful indeed. We look forward to continuing to bring our project to fruition with the same strong, positive spirit begun in Virginia."

Implementing Humanities Action Plans

The twenty-five college teams spent the next eight months thoroughly immersed in meeting their commitments to the *Advancing the Humanities* project by engaging in a wide variety of on- and off-campus activities, including site visits. They communicated their progress throughout the year by means of the *ADVANCING THE HUMANITIES NEWS*. Progress reports received by project staff at AACJC are evidence that this year's participants were fully committed to the completion of the tasks they set for themselves at the National Humanities Conference.

Specifically, less than a month after attending the National Humanities Conference, one team reported that its members had already begun working on a marketing brochure to announce the College's new humanities initiative. In addition, they had met with the entire

George Vaughan, George Mason University, speaks at Humanities Forum at AACJC Convention. Other panelists are, left to right, Lucille Stoddard, Utah Valley Community College, Judith Jeffrey Howard, NEH, and Diane U. Eisenberg, AACJC project manager and panel moderator.

counseling staff of the College to ensure their support as well as with the academic vice president to apprise him of the Airlie experience.

Before the end of the spring 1990 semester, still another college had surveyed the entire faculty to determine the degree of campus-wide support and interest in their humanities project, and had secured the commitment of four visiting scholars for fall faculty study programs. Many of the colleges immediately established detailed schedules and set up specific agendas for campus meetings to implement the new humanities projects. It is clear that this year's *Advancing the Humanities* college teams, as one group reported, "plunged into the tasks they had outlined with their mentor." Having come away from the National Humanities Conference energized and enthusiastic, they began at once "formal and informal efforts to inject colleagues with that enthusiasm."

Year One Accomplishments

Meanwhile, the twenty-four colleges that participated in the first year of the *Advancing the Humanities* project have made great strides in accomplishing their various goals. A number of colleges have designed core courses in ethics and values. Other colleges, recognizing a need for a multicultural focus within the humanities, have designed courses with a global orientation. Still others concentrated their attention on establishing closer ties between the humanities and technology. Descriptions of some of these accomplishments, with excerpts from syllabi and course outlines, have been included in this report to stimulate additional efforts at broadening the range of humanities offerings at community colleges across the nation. (See Part VI.)

AACJC's Humanities Initiative to Continue

Most recently, AACJC, with additional funding from NEH in the amount of $367,795, has launched a new two-year project entitled *Developing Regional Humanities Networks*. It is being conducted in cooperation with the Community College Humanities Association.

The *Developing Regional Humanities Networks* project, spelled out in detail in Part VII of this report, is being directed by James F. Gollattscheck, AACJC executive vice president. Diane U. Eisenberg serves as project manager, and Diana Metcalf is project coordinator. It is anticipated that this new initiative will yield striking benefits for the full spectrum of two-year colleges, enabling colleges with less experience in humanities programming to come into direct, regular contact with nearby colleges that are further along. It will provide opportunities for humanities faculty to share information, problems, support, and services with their colleagues close to home, as they work collaboratively to advance humanities education on their respective campuses.

Part IV
EXEMPLARY HUMANITIES PROJECTS: CASE STUDIES

IN HIS REMARKABLE CELEBRATION OF AMERICAN LIFE and values, *Growing Up*, Russell Baker observes, "We all come from the past, and children ought to know what it was that went into their making, to know that life is a braided cord of humanity stretching up from time long gone." It is clear from reading the *Advancing the Humanities* case studies described in the following pages that the nation's community colleges believe that such knowledge should be made available to students of all ages, not only to children. They have been working hard at ensuring that their students "know what it was that went into their making," as they develop innovative and challenging new ways in which to demonstrate that no matter how geographically and demographically diverse our individual backgrounds, through the study of the humanities, including the great books of many cultures, we can learn that all of us are a part of that "braided cord of humanity."

Of the following eight projects, each of which was originally developed with the assistance of NEH Higher Education in the Humanities grants, the first three are new to the *Advancing the Humanities* mentor program this year. These three, from Kirkwood Community College, Nassau Community College, and Prince George's Community College, join the others in having been carefully designed to provide rigorous intellectual stimulation and pleasure to both students and faculty through the study of the humanities in a manner best suited to the needs of the specific institution.

Kirkwood Community College
Cedar Rapids, Iowa

In 1979, like most community colleges at the time, Kirkwood Community College offered students a "cafeteria" approach to the humanities. They could fulfill graduation requirements by taking any two or more of sixty courses. As a result, students were taking fewer and fewer humanities courses, and their selections were seriously imbalanced. Over a period of years, and with the assistance of a series of National Endowment for the Humanities grants, the College significantly strengthened its Associate Degree program. At the same time, the College became aware of the need for faculty development activities and instituted a series of summer seminars for faculty. As a result, communication and cooperation between humanities faculty and administration improved markedly, and many faculty experienced intellectual renewal.

Gradually, as its vision became sharper and bolder, Kirkwood began to talk more about humanities education for all college students, and discussions took place between humanities and career education faculty and administration. The goal was to create a number of humanities courses of special interest and value to career students and to encourage continued humanities faculty development and cooperation while focusing especially on career education faculty.

Specifically, a 1988–91 NEH grant entitled "Integrating Humanities into Career Education" is allowing Kirkwood to accomplish the following:

- develop three interdisciplinary humanities courses focusing on topics of special interest to career education students;
- establish three six-week summer seminars over three consecutive summers for career education and humanities faculty who will be teaching the new courses; the topics are "Working in America," "Technology and the Human Condition," and "Living in the Information Age";
- improve communication and cooperation between career education and humanities faculty;
- create a new full-time humanities position;
- acquire additional library materials to support the new program;
- disseminate information about the program to other education institutions.

A committee of both humanities and career education faculty developed a generic syllabus from which both faculty summer seminars and interdisciplinary courses are drawing. Among some of the works examined are Arthur Miller's *Death of a Salesman*, Studs Terkel's *Working*, W.E.B. Du Bois' *The Souls of Black Folk*, Henry David Thoreau's *Walden*, and selections from the Bible, Franz Kafka, Karl Marx, Thomas Jefferson, Thomas Aquinas, and Plato, as well as songs, poems, and works of visual art.

Justifiably proud of their accomplishments, directors Joseph Collins and Robert Sessions aver: "Our work on these NEH projects has been highly rewarding. Preparation for and writing of the grant application, as well as the activities of the grant, have helped us clarify and strengthen our curriculum and our individual courses; and our faculty have gained immeasurably as individuals and as a group. For us, the NEH grant process has functioned like opening night for an actor—it has encouraged and prodded us to perform well."

The following is an excerpt from Kirkwood's course outline for "Introduction to Humanities: Working in America"

Other Voices: Experiences and Values of Work

The purpose of this section is to enrich the student's understanding of the place of work in human life by exploring some of the ways in which work has been presented through various artifacts. Topics included in this section are education and work, work as a curse, the celebration of work, materialism, conformity and rebellion, consumerism, the family and work, alienation, and the city/country conflict.

A. Introduction to the Multiplicity of Work Values

1. Arthur Miller, *Death of a Salesman.* This classic play (we will use the Dustin Hoffman version of the movie) reflects most of the issues that this section and much of the rest of the course are about.
2. Interviews from Studs Terkel's *Working.* Selections from this book make good reading for each topic in this section.
3. Songs: "Heigh Ho," "Whistle While You Work"; "Take This Job and Shove It"; "Forty Hour Week"; work songs from the sea; songs of slaves.

B. The Yin-Yang of Work: Our Ambivalent Attitudes Toward Work

1. Donald Hall, "The Man in the Dead Machine." In this satiric poem Hall is concerned with how some work in the modern world can diminish human life.
2. Robert Frost, "Mowing." This is a poetic exploration of modern work as a source of limited but significant meaning.
3. Robert Frost, "A Tuft of Flowers." Frost celebrates work which is done in a community of fellow workers.
4. Judeo-Christian readings which celebrate and/or question the value of work. Genesis 2-3; Amos 6:18, 9:2-7; Matthew 6:19-34, 7:1-12.
5. Representations of work in the art of Courbet, Millet, Hine, Avedon, and Grant Wood.
6. Songs: "Working Girl Blues" (Leona Williams); "Speedball Tucker" (Jim Croce).

Nassau Community College
Garden City, New York

"A Time to Think About Shakespeare" is an apt description of the NEH-sponsored humanities project developed by Nassau Community College (NCC) under the direction of Bernice W. Kliman. According to Kliman, although faculty at the College all acknowledged the need to study Shakespeare, they also "needed time to think about the plays." For most, the pressure of teaching four classes each semester offered little opportunity for reading academic journals and keeping up with the latest in Shakespeare scholarship and teaching strategies. They especially needed to discover ways to engage NCC students. The 22,000 students came to the campus with a wide range of needs, experiences, and goals. The NCC faculty study group, "A Time to Think About Shakespeare," was formed to provide the intellectual basis for revitalization of the teaching of Shakespeare at the College and to address a number of related issues:

- the problem of teaching Shakespeare to students who find the material extremely difficult;
- the need to make connections between Shakespeare and contemporary concerns;
- the distance of faculty from their own graduate training in Shakespeare and from current critical theories which could affect teaching strategies;
- the need for a scholarly forum through which faculty could exchange intellectual experiences in order to promote individual and group motivation and confidence in the teaching of a variety of Shakespeare's plays.

The study group of twenty-six fulltime faculty members, which met for over fifty hours in June 1989, was designed to meet these needs. Each week, a master mentor directed the activities of the study group and suggested assignments and project ideas to participants, centering on performance issues. Maurice Charney, Distinguished Professor of English, Rutgers University, led the group's discussion of *Hamlet.* During their examination of *Antony and Cleopatra,* the group worked with Professor Ralph Cohen, Department of English, James Madison University. Lynda Boose, associate professor of English, Dartmouth College, directed the examination of *The Tempest.*

Other visiting scholars introduced such issues as performance as interpretation, post new-critical concerns related to performance and non-authoritarian teaching, and actors in the classroom. Each participant worked on an individual project with a master mentor; all twenty-six participants continued to meet as a group through monthly brown-bag luncheon/discussions the following year to exchange ideas on classroom application of seminar discoveries. Mentors continue to make themselves available for consultation.

Project director Kliman maintains that through its Shakespeare study group, Nassau Community College "saved Shakespeare as a course of study." Faculty were freed from preconceived notions of teaching and understanding Shakespeare and developed the enthusiasm and confidence to employ new techniques and explore a variety of ways of communicating with their students.

According to Sean Fanelli, president, Nassau Community College, "The *Advancing the Humanities* program has allowed us a chance to share our Shakespeare project with others—but also to learn from others. It has been a mutually enriching experience."

The following is an example of a classroom strategy developed for the Shakespeare study group at Nassau Community College

Directions for student group work—*Hamlet*, Act I, scene ii

1. Choose a recorder from among you. This person will read the rest of these directions aloud to the group. The recorder should simply jot down some notes about decisions, as briefly as possible, and also take part in the discussion, which he or she will report on after the performances. The recorder should also be a performer.

2. Decide which part of the court scene you'd like to focus on and why. You can use the whole segment or any part of it.

3. Cast the scene from among you.

4. Decide what your overall aim is: what are the points you want to make?

   What adjective would best describe your image of Claudius?

   Of Gertrude? Of Laertes? Of Hamlet?

   What do you want the audience to think while or after they see this segment?

5. Each actor may work out, with the group, a paraphrase for the lines. Others can help by referring to the text. Alternatively, you may read the lines. And you may also mix paraphrases with Shakespeare's language.

6. Everyone in the group should try out where to stand for the segment and where to move (blocking). Everyone should have some role, even if he or she doesn't have a speaking part. Be a *working* supernumerary, that is, a bystander who helps to get the point across.

   Here are some questions to consider: Is Ophelia present?

   The first folio says she is; the second quarto omits her.

   What's the difference?

   When should the audience become aware of Hamlet? What is he doing while others are speaking?

   How would you have the characters enter, or would you have them "discovered" on stage?

7. Practice what you've decided.

Prince George's Community College
Largo, Maryland

Prince George's Community College is located between Baltimore and Washington, D. C., and is staffed by a tenured, experienced faculty. However, the faculty faces increasingly heavy teaching loads and wide disparities in student competencies, leaving little time for scholarly pursuits.

In 1989, Prince George's sponsored a four-week summer seminar in Greek mythology for humanities faculty under the direction of Isa Engleberg, professor of speech, communication and theater, and currently coordinator of faculty and academic services (Engleberg defines her job as "to do good things for the faculty"). The seminar, designed to fulfill the faculty's need for intellectual renewal and revitalization, was funded by the National Endowment for the Humanities. Entitled "The Nature and Function of Greek Mythology," it provided compensation adequate to free faculty from summer school teaching so that they could concentrate their efforts on the study of Greek mythology.

The seminar was conducted by Bernard M. Knox, director emeritus, Center for Hellenic Studies in Washington, D. C., whose lectures were augmented by a series of presentations by distinguished classics scholars. The seminar focused on understanding the essence of mythology, its purposes and functions in Greek society, and the application of the study of myth to a variety of intellectual disciplines.

The first week of the month-long seminar offered a review of modern approaches to Greek mythology: Freudian, Jungian, structuralist, linguistic, and anthropological. The lectures, films, and discussions in week two centered on the function of myth in Greek society. The third week, as well as each afternoon of the entire seminar, was set aside for individual research and seminar project preparation, with the opportunity for consultations with Knox. In the final week of the seminar, participants studied the influence of Greek mythology on Western literature and art. All participants prepared papers on related subjects reflecting individual discipline interests.

Final projects reflected the broad range of interests of seminar participants. Papers explored such diverse areas as "A Comparison of Greek Mythology with Finno-Ugric Myths," "Greek Mythology and Science Fiction," "Myth in the Cold War," "Mythic Elements in

Masks & Myths

PRESENTATIONS ON GREEK MYTHOLOGY

FORUM I— Greek Myth: Gods, Men, and Women

OCTOBER 31, 1990

Nobility Seduced: Women and Ladies in The Odyssey
The Rennie Forum, 7:30 p.m.
Dr. Victoria Pedrick, Associate Professor of Classics at Georgetown University, will discuss the roles of women—both common and noble—in Homeric culture, and their relationship to the larger warrior society of ancient Greece.

NOVEMBER 28, 1990

Ariadne's Thread: Classical Mythology and Contemporary Poetry
The Rennie Forum, 3:00 p.m.
Dr. Dale Sinos, Associate Professor and Chair of Classics at Howard University, will read and discuss modern poetry as influenced by the themes and characters of Greek mythology.

DECEMBER 5, 1990

Greek Drama on Film
The Rennie Forum, 3:00 p.m.
Mr. Jay Schlossberg-Cohen, Director of the Maryland Film Commission, and Mr. Edward Cockrell, Director of Film Programming at the American Film Institute, will discuss contemporary film versions of Greek dramas (*Medea, Iphigenia, The Trojan Women*).

FORUM II— Greek Myth: Then and Now

FEBRUARY 20, 1991

Classics Unbound
The Rennie Forum, 7:30 p.m.
Dr. Sheila Murnaghan, Associate Professor of Classics at the University of Pennsylvania, will explain how the literature of a Western, male-dominated, and warlike society can have value and meaning for people of diverse social and cultural backgrounds.

FEBRUARY 27, 1991

Reflections of Ancient Greece in America
The Rennie Forum, 3:00 p.m.
Dr. Wilford Scott, lecturer in the Education Department of the National Gallery of Art, will present a lecture and slide presentation on how America's artistic vision is rooted in the ideals and art of ancient Greece.

MARCH 20, 1991

The Light of the Gods
The Rennie Forum, 3:00 p.m.
Through film and lecture, Ms. Judith Andraka, chair of the Prince George's Community College Art Department, will discuss how the Greek artists of the 6th century B.C. reflected the new philosophy of and interest in "man as the measure of all things."

FORUM III— Greek Myth: New Perspectives

APRIL 3, 1991

Discovering Myths: Language, Culture, and Self
The Rennie Forum, 3:00 p.m.
Dr. Joseph O'Connor, Associate Professor of Classics at Georgetown University, will discuss how myth transmits cultures and promotes a sense of community. Dr. O'Connor will focus on the links between traditional tales and education.

APRIL 10, 1991

A Platonic Symposium: Modern Issues in Ancient Myth
The Rennie Forum, 3:00 p.m.
Prince George's Community College faculty will explore how Greek myth can be taught and enjoyed in light of contemporary social issues: the celebration of cultural diversity, the horror of modern warfare, development of contemporary literature.

APRIL 17, 1991

The Iliad: A War Poem Brought to Life
The Rennie Forum, 3:00 & 7:30 p.m.
Dr. Alan Wade, Associate Professor of Theatre at The George Washington University, will interpret passages from *The Iliad* based on Dr. Bernard Knox's lecture "The Iliad as a War Poem." Dr. Wade will recreate the clash between Greeks and Trojans immortalized in this epic poem.

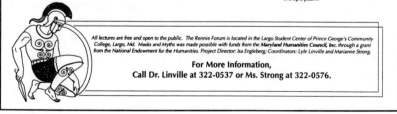

*All lectures are free and open to the public. The Rennie Forum is located in the Largo Student Center of Prince George's Community College, Largo, Md. Masks and Myths was made possible with funds from the **Maryland Humanities Council, Inc.** through a grant from the National Endowment for the Humanities. Project Director: Isa Engleberg; Coordinators: Lyle Linville and Marianne Strong.*

**For More Information,
Call Dr. Linville at 322-0537 or Ms. Strong at 322-0576.**

Prince George's Community College announces a lecture series on Greek mythology, open to the public as well as to students.

Rational Thought," "Circe: From Fantasy to Nightmare," and "Mythic Echoes in Contemporary Teenage Fiction."

The Greek mythology project at Prince George's Community College gave birth to a wealth of additional activities and generated both intellectual excitement and collegiality on the campus. Following the seminar, a series of luncheon lectures on mythology were organized, featuring a well-attended public lecture by Knox on "The *Iliad*: A War Poem." The instructional area newsletter *Instructional Forum* began a regular column entitled "Mythoskepsis," a newly coined word meaning "looking at myth," in which seminar participants described their research projects. Several seminar papers were published; others were presented at discipline and pedagogical conferences including a panel at the 1990 Community College Humanities Association regional conference in New York.

The Greek mythology project also inspired two subsequent grant-funded activities. The Maryland Humanities Council funded nine public lectures on Greek mythology featuring university scholars and members of the Prince George's Community College faculty. The National Endowment for the Humanities funded a statewide summer seminar on the college campus open to twenty-two Maryland community college faculty entitled "The Greek Experiment," to explore the foundations of the humanities in Western civilization—the history, literature, and philosophy of the ancient Greeks—concentrating on the fifth century B.C. Study will be organized around the Greek "inventions" of democracy, drama, and ethics, and will be conducted by Donald Kagan, dean, Yale College, Alfonso Gomez-Lobo, professor of philosophy, Georgetown University, and Bernard Knox.

The initial Prince George's Community College Greek mythology proposal described the goals of the project as creating a greater emphasis on the importance of scholarship in planning and developing course materials; increasing the status of participants as scholar-educators for other faculty; and enhancing student awareness of the importance of Greek mythology in our culture. All of the faculty participants are convinced that their expectations were realistic and that the goals continue to be met in new and unexpected ways, long after the completion of the seminar. In fact, states President Robert I. Bickford:

"The NEH-funded Greek mythology project has transformed our humanities faculty into productive humanities scholars. The seminar and its follow-up activities have demonstrated how a commitment to faculty scholarship can improve faculty morale and instruction, while better serving the entire college community. In less than two years, Prince George's Community College has become a new mecca for humanities programming in Maryland."

The following is the schedule for Prince George's faculty seminar

"The Greek Experiment," June 3–28, 1991
Week One, June 3–7
  Mon., a.m.: Orientation, Lycurgus and Spartan Constitution; p.m.: Campus tour
  Tues., a.m.: Periclean Democracy; p.m.: *Antigone*
  Wed., a.m.: The Function of the Polis; p.m.: Group discussion
  Thurs., a.m.: The Peloponnesian War; p.m.: *Medea*
  Fri.: Individual research
Week Two, June 10–14
  Mon., a.m.: Homer to Pindar: p.m.: *Oedipus Rex*
  Tues., a.m.: Tragedy and Comedy; p.m.: National Gallery
  Wed., a.m.: Modern Poems and Classical Themes; p.m.: Group discussion
  Thurs., a.m.: Prose and Literature as a National Identity; p.m.: *Iphigenia*
  Fri., Individual research
Week Three, June 17–21
  Research and Writing, Consultation with Knox
Week Four, June 24–28
  Mon., a.m.: The Invention of Ethics; p.m.: The Athens of Socrates
  Tues., a.m.: Moral Philosophy; p.m.: Walters Art Gallery
  Wed., a.m.: Pre-Socratic Philosophy; p.m.: Group discussion
  Thurs., a.m.: *Eudaimonia* as the Basis of Ethics
  Fri., p.m.: Luncheon

Community College of Philadelphia
Philadelphia, Pennsylvania

The Community College of Philadelphia, the second largest community college in the state, is an urban institution which has a current enrollment of over 35,000. The student population is ethnically diverse, fifty-one percent black, forty percent white, nine percent Asian, Hispanic, and other ethnic groups. Fifty percent of these are from economically disadvantaged backgrounds. Although they are rich in life experience, they often have had limited contact with significant literary and historical texts as well as little exposure to many of the central ideas of Western culture.

These same students are unable to devote themselves to full-time study because of economic need or family responsibilities. Over the past five years, the part-time student population has increased dramatically. Many part-time students enroll in only one course per semester, and their most common choice is introductory English composition.

To meet the needs of these students and their faculty, who are often part-time as well, the Community College of Philadelphia, under the leadership of Karen Bojar and Grace Flisser, developed the "Cultural Literacy Project" to strengthen English composition courses offered to part-time students in the evenings, on weekends, or at off-campus sites by adding significant works of literature and history to the courses.

Just as part-time students tend to lack the usual array of support services, part-time faculty miss the usual opportunities for faculty development. A five-week summer institute for part-time teachers of part-time students was created to ensure that faculty had the opportunity to develop strategies for integrating historically and culturally relevant information with in-depth analysis of key literary and historical texts and to explore ways of using such texts as the basis for writing assignments for their part-time students. The ultimate goal was to transform introductory English composition from courses which involve a heterogeneous mixture of pedagogies and materials to courses which center on the concept of cultural literacy.

Faculty attending the institute continued to meet the following semester to discuss the classroom utility of ideas and strategies developed as a result of the institute and to modify and refine their

25

ideas and materials as needed in order to present them to a wider audience. They presented their ideas at annual meetings of professional associations such as the Community College Humanities Association and at a regional conference on cultural literacy organized by the directors of the project.

The project drew upon the expertise of faculty involved in three humanities programs offered on the main campus of the College during the day: an honors program originally funded by NEH and now funded entirely by the College; a transfer opportunities program in which students received intensive educational experience based on the exploration of primary sources and involvement in a community of learners; and linked humanities courses developed as a result of an NEH grant for another summer institute which brought together ten teams of humanities teachers who designed a linked English composition course and humanities curriculum.

The "Cultural Literacy Project" summer institute for faculty was held for a five-week period, four days a week. Participants began by exploring the theoretical implications of the concept of cultural literacy and read materials on the subject by E. D. Hirsch, as well as by some thoughtful respondents to his position. They also focused on tactics for presenting appropriate humanities texts so that students perceive them as central to their lives. Later, they considered groups of texts which might form the core of an English composition class and considered the ways in which different combinations of readings might prove effective.

Commencing with the third week of the institute, participants began to focus on a series of texts organized thematically. Thus, they began with an examination of the Calvinist tradition from the vantage point of female experience and read Nancy Cott's *The Bonds of Womanhood: Women's Sphere in New England* and *The Captivity and Restoration of Mrs. Mary Rowlandson,* Nathaniel Hawthorne's *The Scarlet Letter,* and Arthur Miller's *The Crucible.* For an exploration of the role of women in nineteenth-century America in the broader context of the struggle for human rights, faculty were required to read Sarah Moore Grimke's *Letters on the Equality of the Sexes* and *The Condition of Women,* Elizabeth Cady Stanton's *Eighty Years and More* and *Diary and Reminiscences, The Narrative of the Life of Frederick Douglass,* and Henry David Thoreau's "A Plea for Captain John Brown."

Week four of the institute covered the history of racial relations in U.S. history, particularly as represented in literary academic texts. Required reading was Mark Twain's *Huckleberry Finn*, Leo Marx's "Mr. Eliot, Mr. Trilling, and Huckleberry Finn," Ralph Ellison's *Invisible Man* and "Change the Joke and Slip the Yoke," and Oscar Handlin's *Race and Nationality in American Life*.

On the theme of economic dislocation in the 1930's, texts considered were John Steinbeck's *Grapes of Wrath*, Zora Neale Hurston's *Their Eyes Were Watching God*, James T. Farrell's *The Young Lonigan*, and Dorothea Lange and P. S. Taylor's *An American Exodus*.

The final week of the institute was devoted to works which look at the U. S. experience from an international perspective: *In Our Time* by Hemingway, *Hiroshima* by John Hersey, *The Great War and Modern Memory* by Paul Fussell, and Theodore Roosevelt's "How We Acquired the Panama Canal" and selections from *Rough Riders*.

As a result of the successful completion of the first institute, the regional conference, and the positive publicity surrounding the full range of project activities, a second group of faculty were recruited for another five-week institute. Although format, reading list, and guest speakers were essentially the same, some modifications were made in light of participants' comments and an outside evaluator's assessment.

The Community College of Philadelphia is confident that its "Cultural Literacy Project" is playing an important role in heightening student awareness of the crucial place of widely shared humanities information in a literate society and encouraging students to examine the political and social implications of the kind of knowledge base the "culturally literate" are assumed to possess. It is also strengthening collegiality between full- and part-time faculty, and those on and off campus, through the interchange of ideas and shared experiences.

The following is an excerpt of a syllabus from one of the Community College of Philadelphia's new composition courses

Required Texts:

Habits of the Heart: Individualism and Commitment in American Life by Robert N. Bellah et al.

Walden and "Civil Disobedience" by Henry David Thoreau

Selections from *Democracy in America* by Alexis de Tocqueville

Autobiography by Benjamin Franklin

"Self-Reliance" and other essays by Ralph Waldo Emerson

"Song of Myself," *Leaves of Grass,* by Walt Whitman

"Letter from a Birmingham Jail" and "The Social Organization of Non-Violence" by Martin Luther King, Jr.

Course Description:

In order to develop the kinds of writing skills you will need to succeed in college, you must develop your ability to analyze and respond to sophisticated texts. Most of the writing assignments for this semester will be based on a group of texts which explore the tradition of individualism in American life.

Weeks One and Two:

We will work backwards and begin with a contemporary theme. The article "Heroes for Hard Times" describes several individuals who have chosen to make a commitment to work to improve their communities. We will discuss how common such choices are in our society and what our society does to encourage or discourage such behavior.

In a journal, you will keep a record of your reaction to the various readings. The notes you take will be the raw material you will draw upon for the essay assignments. You will write several drafts for each essay and receive a grade for each draft. Journals will be collected periodically but will not be graded.

Jefferson State Community College
Birmingham, Alabama

Jefferson State Community College is one of the largest public two-year colleges in Alabama. It is a commuter institution in the northeastern section of Birmingham, serving an enrollment of 6,095 students. The College has recently undergone a dramatic change in the makeup of its student body. In the past, students were for the most part of average academic ability and only marginally prepared for college work. Thus, faculty were rarely intellectually challenged or felt the need to increase their own knowledge for the benefit of their students. In addition, limited financial resources available to the College left little opportunity for supporting faculty interest in advanced study or participation in professional meetings. These factors resulted in serious cases of burnout among many humanities faculty, almost all of whom had been teaching at Jefferson State for over fifteen years.

Recently, however, the College has enrolled an increasing number of academically talented students and has been actively working to develop an honors program. The honors program, which began in the fall of 1986, now offers opportunities for the humanities faculty to become involved in intellectually stimulating interdisciplinary humanities courses. The two-year program includes four five-hour humanities courses combining disciplines within the humanities. The courses are team taught and present a sequential study of the major ideas and development of Western civilization within a historical framework. The courses are designed to introduce students to the great works of Western civilization and to help them understand their literary, historical, and artistic heritage. Course instructors present the materials thematically whenever possible to illustrate the interrelations of art, literature, music, philosophy, and history and the variety of ways in which they reflect cultural values.

Under the direction of Agnes Pollock, Jefferson State designed and conducted a project entitled "Faculty Renewal and Development Through Interdisciplinary Humanities Seminars," which was funded by the National Endowment for the Humanities. The project's goals were twofold: to combat faculty burnout by providing opportunities for intellectual growth, and to develop a pool of teachers for the honors program.

The faculty seminars met for one and a half hours twice a week. Each seminar was open to twelve faculty members, who received release time from one class, studied the assigned materials, participated in the analyses of the works, and did research on the reading material for which they were responsible. The required reading for the courses included the major works taught in the humanities honors courses as well as *The Humanities in Western Cultures,* Volumes 1 and 2, a humanities text which provides historical overviews and information on major developments in art, music, and literature.

An important feature of each seminar was the opportunity for participants as well as other interested faculty to hear both local and nationally known scholars address topics related to the subjects studied. Following the presentations, time was set aside for informal discussions between the visiting scholar and the audience.

The faculty seminars began in the winter of 1988, with "The Classical World." Required reading for the course was drawn from among the following works: the *Iliad,* the *Odyssey,* works by Plato, excerpts from Herodotus, Thucydides' *History of the Peloponnesian Wars,* the plays of Aeschylus, Sophocles, Aristophanes, and Euripides, the poetry of Sappho, Aristotle's *Nichomachean Ethics* and *Politics,* the *Odes* of Horace, Ovid's *Art of Love,* Lucretius' *De Rerum Natura,* Juvenal's *Third Satire,* and excerpts from St. Augustine and the Bible. In addition, seminar participants attended lectures by James Rachels, professor of philosophy, University of Alabama, on the Greek concept of virtue; Margaret Boegeman, professor of English, Cypress College, on Greek mythology in art and literature; and Sam Pezzilo, professor of classics, Birmingham-Southern College, on Greek and Roman architecture.

The second semester, held in the spring of 1988, covered "The Medieval World and the Renaissance." For this course, faculty participants read excerpts from Aquinas and Chaucer, *The Song of Roland, Tristan and Iseult, Sir Gawaine and the Green Knight,* Malory, T. E. White's *The Once and Future King,* Dante, Boccaccio, Erasmus' *In Praise of Folly,* Machiavelli's *The Prince,* and viewed appropriate films and videos. Scholarly presentations were made by Susan Hagan on "The World of Chaucer through Art"; Flowers Braswell on "Arthurian Legend"; James Wilhelm on Dante; and Michael McInturff on Renaissance art and culture.

"The Neo-Classical Age and the Romantic Rebellion" was the title of the third seminar offered the following winter. The course covered Thomas Hobbes' *Leviathan,* Blaise Pascal's *Thoughts: an Apology for Christianity,* Jean Baptiste Racine's *Phaedra, Essay Concerning Human Understanding* by John Locke, Alexander Pope's "An Essay on Man," Jonathan Swift's "Modest Proposal," Goethe's *Faust* Part I, poems by William Wordsworth, Percy Bysshe Shelley, Samuel Coleridge, Lord Byron, and John Keats, Shelley's *Prometheus Unbound* and *The Cenci, Pride and Prejudice* by Jane Austen, and Mary Wollstonecraft's *Vindication of the Rights of Woman.*

The fourth seminar, "Political and Intellectual Forces in the Modern World," covered works by Friedrich Nietzsche, Karl Marx, Sigmund Freud, Adolf Hitler, W.E.B. Du Bois, Malcolm X, Martin Luther King, Jr., Ernest Hemingway, and Virginia Woolf.

The final seminars of the series were presented in the winter and spring of 1990 and focused on "Creative Forces in the Modern World." Participants explored Feodor Dostoevsky's *Crime and Punishment,* a short story by Sherwood Anderson, Anton Chekhov's *The Cherry Orchard,* Henrik Ibsen, George Bernard Shaw, Samuel Beckett, selected poems of Robert Frost, William Butler Yeats, Dylan Thomas, and e e cummings, excerpts from Hans Bonhoffer, works of Albert Camus, Franz Kafka, T. S. Eliot, Langston Hughes' poems and short stories, Bernard Malamud's *The Magic Barrel,* Antoine Saint Exupery's *The Little Prince,* James Joyce's *Dubliners,* and William Faulkner's "A Rose for Emily" and *As I Lay Dying.*

The faculty seminars have been enthusiastically received by Jefferson State participants. Many applauded the interdisciplinary nature of the discussions; said one faculty member, "Being involved in scholarly discussions with colleagues outside my discipline was an interesting and refreshing change."

Although some participants expressed frustration at the length and number of reading assignments, most were delighted to have the opportunity to share in the experience. Enthusiasm for the interdisciplinary approach and the intellectual renewal was reflected in the following comments: "The seminars provided the opportunity for conversations which I have long wished could be going on in hallways and our offices"; "Many of us talked about the material outside the seminar—probably to the point that we frustrated colleagues who were not participating"; "A general bravo for the idea—the kind of thing that is positive and brings us together in the only really important way—for learning together and for enjoying the process and for inspiring each other."

According to Jefferson State president Judy Merritt, the goals have been met: "During the past three years faculty have had the opportunity to read, research, and engage one another intellectually in a series of interdisciplinary seminars. They have also benefited from the presentations of numerous outstanding scholars from other colleges and universities. To a great extent humanities faculty who have participated fully in these seminars have overcome their previous burnout; they are more eager and better prepared to teach their classes. Another major benefit of this project is that more faculty are willing and prepared to teach our recently developed interdisciplinary honors courses."

Jefferson State Community College is convinced that its humanities project will have a long-term positive impact on students as well as on faculty. Obviously, what seminar participants learned in the courses they were able to pass directly on to their students. But even more, the intellectual revitalization experienced by seminar participants increased their enthusiasm for teaching and gave them the confidence to want to teach the honors courses. Jefferson State expects to see an increased interest among its faculty in an integrated approach to learning as well as growing faculty interest in designing additional humanities honors courses and redesigning some current courses with a more interdisciplinary approach in mind. Perhaps the following comment from a faculty member best sums up the success of Jefferson State's "Faculty Renewal and Development Through Interdisciplinary Humanities Seminars" project: "It was a pleasure and a thrill to see myself and other sufferers of burnout rediscover the job of scholarship, the heady exchange of ideas, and the refinement of perspective that comes from enlightened debate."

The following is the reading list for Jefferson State Community College's sixth "Faculty Renewal" seminar

Seminar VI: Creative Forces in the Modern World

The Writer as Existential Philosopher:
Jean Paul Sartre, *No Exit,* "The Wall"
Samuel Beckett, *Waiting for Godot*
Franz Kafka, selected short stories
Albert Camus, *The Stranger,* "The Myth of Sisyphus"
20th Century Experimentation: Time, Space, and Form:
William Butler Yeats, selected poems
James Joyce, selected stories from *Dubliners*
T.S. Eliot, "Prufrock," "The Hollow Men," *The Waste Land*
William Faulkner, "A Rose for Emily," *As I Lay Dying*
Katherine A. Porter, "The Jilting of Granny Weatherall" and   other
    short stories
Lawrence Durrell, *Justine* and other novels from *Alexandria Quartet*
e e cummings, selected poems
Celebration of Enduring Human Values:
Langston Hughes, selected poems and Jesse Simple stories
Dylan Thomas, selected poems and stories
Antoine St. Exupery, *The Little Prince*
Bernard Malamud, "The Magic Barrel" and other short stories
Other Voices:
Eudora Welty, *The Ponder Heart* and/or "The Petrified Man," "Why
    I Live at the P.O." and other stories
Toni Cade Bambara, "The Lesson" and other stories
Doris Lessing, "The Black Madonna" and other stories
Denise Levertov, selected poems
Non-Literary Material:
Cubism (video—"The Shock of the New")
Modern architecture—Louis Sullivan, Frank Lloyd Wright and
    others (videos)
Modern dance—works by Martha Graham, Alvin Ailey and others
    (videos)
Art of Marc Chagall and Henri Matisse
Development of jazz—guest speaker
Music by George Gershwin and Aaron Copland
Experimental music of Arnold Schonberg, John Cage and others

Piedmont Virginia Community College
Charlottesville, Virginia

"As nothing before it, our College's humanities project, which began with an NEH Planning Grant, has helped us better grapple with the multiple relationships among the multiple realities of our curriculum and its teaching. It has challenged us to forge better linkages between our occupational/technical program and our general education program. It has encouraged us to think about cross-disciplines. And it has moved us toward a better balance between career and life—for both ourselves and our students."

Deborah M. DiCroce, president
Piedmont Virginia Community College

Piedmont Virginia Community College is located in central Virginia just outside Charlottesville. The College offers college-transfer programs, pre-college developmental education, community services, and a variety of occupational/technical programs. From an enrollment of 462 students in 1972, the College's population had grown to 4,139 by 1986. Piedmont enjoys a close relationship with the University of Virginia, which is three miles away. Approximately sixty of the College's students transfer to the University each year. Mary Baldwin College of Stanton, Virginia, conducts an adult-degree program at several locations around the state, including the Piedmont Campus. Because of the university-oriented nature of the community surrounding the College, a large proportion of the students are enrolled in college transfer programs. Sixty percent of the degree-seeking students enroll in programs leading to the Associate in Arts or the Associate in Science degree.

In light of its academic orientation, it is logical that Piedmont should focus its attention on defining and stressing the importance of general education for all its students. The College had been studying ways to strengthen its humanities program. An NEH planning grant, in 1986–87, enabled the College to review the state of the humanities on its campus, assessing courses offered, degree requirements, library facilities, extracurricular activities, and faculty development programs. The project herein described, "Strengthening General Education Through the Humanities," under the direction of Evelyn Edson, derived from the findings of that study.

To begin with, it was determined that at least three credits in the humanities would be required for the Associate Degree in all of the College's programs. To help satisfy the requirement, Piedmont designed an interdisciplinary and team-taught core humanities course. The course, taught by four humanities faculty members, is offered each semester. Materials include a section on ancient Greece, with required reading of the *Odyssey, Oedipus Rex,* Plato's *Symposium,* Greek lyric poetry, an examination of Greek vases, *Antigone,* Plautus' *Menaechmi,* Plutarch's *Parallel Lives,* and the Bible, as well as a study of the medieval cathedral and its association with music, drama, and philosophy. The course also includes Shakespeare and examines Raphael's Stanze della Segnatura and Michelangelo's Sistine ceiling as works of art and as philosophical statements. Renaissance music, both secular and religious, and Bach's *Saint Matthew Passion* are on the program, as are Mozart's *Magic Flute* and symphonies of Beethoven, Stravinsky and Debussy. Readings include Goethe's *Faust,* Jane Austen, Thomas Mann, Virginia Woolf, and the poetry of T.S. Eliot and William Butler Yeats.

Piedmont's core humanities course encompasses art, music, literature, and philosophy. Now in its fourth year, it has some one hundred students in four sections and is prospering. A humanities teacher recalls comments from students after a field trip to the museum to examine the Greek vase collection: "When I heard that we were going to write on Greek vases, I thought, *never.* But we did, and I did." Said another, "I fell in love with my vase."

To ensure continued faculty commitment to the humanities and to encourage intellectual exchange and a deeper sense of community among the faculty, a series of summer seminars were established to run for three consecutive years. The seminars are open to fifteen faculty members at a time and are held in conjunction with the Center for the Liberal Arts, University of Virginia. The first of the intensive three-week seminars was held in 1989. Tibor Wlassics, professor of Italian languages and literature, focused on Dante's *Inferno.* The next seminar, on Plato, was held in 1990 and conducted by Daniel T. Devereux, associate professor of philosophy, University of Virginia. The 1991 seminar involved an interdisciplinary study, "What Is the Baroque?" conducted by scholars in music and art history. Established in 1984, the Center, under the direction of Harold Kolb, has dedicated its efforts to developing partnerships between the University and local school systems. Piedmont is the first community college to work with the Center.

The summer seminars were designed to bring the humanities to a wide group of faculty, provide links with the core course, and offer an opportunity for faculty to meet together to discuss ideas. Participants have an opportunity to be reintroduced to the great works of the humanities and to study them in their cultural and historical context. From a written evaluation of the Dante seminar came the following: "This class has been a pure joy . . . it has been an experience that has changed my life in several ways. The *Divine Comedy* itself is new to me, but now, because of the visions and interpretations of Tibor Wlassics to which I've been exposed, I have a new way of looking at my world. My challenge at Piedmont is to teach science, and what science is, to students who come to me with an impression that it is very dry and sterile. I must show that it is, in the right hands, very creative and beautiful. Tibor has helped me to learn to do this by bridging the gap in the other direction, pointing out how to appreciate great literature, when my background is a scientific one."

Piedmont has developed a number of other activities and programs as part of its "Strengthening General Education Through the Humanities" project. To encourage a humanities perspective in non-humanities classes, faculty development workshops on the humanities core course as well as the summer seminars are open to all full-time and adjunct faculty. Furthermore, the school has opened a new permanent position in philosophy/religion. Course enrollments in this area of the humanities have been steadily increasing, and the College is convinced that sufficient student interest can sustain this position.

Another faculty summer program developed as part of Piedmont's humanities project was a workshop combining the study of a major text in the humanities with the study and practice of writing as a means of learning. Twenty faculty from various disciplines read, discussed, and wrote about Henry David Thoreau's *Walden,* using it as a model of observation, recording, and reflection. The workshop was conducted by Professors Richard Harrington and William D. Owen, of Piedmont's English faculty, who co-direct the Central Virginia Writing Project, University of Virginia.

In addition, a humanities advisory committee has been formed to help coordinate efforts in the humanities at the College with the many programs in art, music, and theater in the surrounding community. And finally, NEH funds were used to increase library holdings in the humanities.

Piedmont Virginia Community College aspires to make the humanities a central part of the life of every student on its campus. In the process of doing so, it has instituted a faculty development program which has proven to be an outstanding success. Edson reports: "Our faculty development project was somewhat unusual in that it was based on the idea of general education through the great books for faculty from all disciplines. The group represented all divisions of the College including business, health technologies, science, math, psychology, government, as well as English, Spanish, and history, and this in itself is very exciting. The intellectual excitement was intense, and for most of us, the course was a sort of spiritual experience. We bonded together as a group and continue to seek one another out. As for Dante—and this would be true for almost any great book—each of us found that we could meet it in our own way and at our own level. What would we change? This seems embarrassing, but really I can't think of anything."

The following schedule is distributed to students enrolled in Piedmont's humanities course at the beginning of the semester

Humanities 201—Student Assignment Schedule—Fall 1989

Aug. 31   Introduction: about the course
          The world of the *Odyssey*
Sept. 7   Homer, *Odyssey*, Bks. I-X
          Greek lyric poetry (handout)
          Guest lecturer: William D. Owen
Sept. 14 *Odyssey*, Bks. XI–XIII, XIX–XXIV
          Art lecture: Greek vase painting
          Paper on the *Odyssey*, due Sept. 14
Sept. 21 Sophocles, *Oedipus Rex*
          Introduction to Plato
          Guest lecturer: Kay Bethea
Sept. 24 Field trip to Virginia Museum of Fine Arts, Richmond
          Museum paper due Oct. 5
Sept. 28 Plato, *Symposium*
          Art lecture: classicism (the Parthenon)
          Guest lecturer: Marietta McCarty
Oct. 5   Old Testament: Psalms 1, 8, 23, 100
          Job, all but chs. 32–37
          Film: *Heritage: Civilization and the Jews*
Oct. 12   New Testament: Matthew (all)
          Selections from Acts and Romans (TBA)
          Guest lecturer: William D. Owen
Oct. 19   Hour exam
Oct. 26   Plutarch, *Life of Cato*
          Art lecture: Roman portraits
Nov. 1   Stoicism: Epictetus, *Handbook*
          Readings in philosophy (St. Thomas Aquinas, Anselm,
              Meister Eckhart), handouts
          Guest lecturer: Marietta McCarty
Nov. 9   Art lecture: Medieval cathedrals
          Drama in the cathedral: *Everyman*
          Medieval music
          Introduction to Dante
          Guest lecturer: Kay Bethea
Nov. 12   Field trip to National Cathedral in Washington, D.C.
          Paper due Nov. 16.
Nov. 16   Dante, *Inferno*
          Giotto, Revolution in art, art lecture
Nov. 30   Renaissance music
          Art lecture, Raphael and Michelangelo
          Reading: Cellini, *Autobiography*, pp. 15–101, 188–232, 312–76
          Guest lecturer: Kay Bethea
Dec. 7   Continue with Cellini
          Poetry: Petrarch's and Shakespeare's sonnets
          Final paper due on the last day of class
Dec. 14   Final exam

Richland College
Dallas, Texas

Richland College is one of seven campuses in the Dallas Community College District. Present enrollment is more than 12,000 full- and part-time students. The College offers the usual range of programs as well as special programs in cooperative education and international studies.

"College Classics Cluster Project: Integrating the Classics into General Education" is the title of the Richland College NEH-supported humanities project, developed and originally directed by Nanette Pascal, now coordinated by Lee Paez. The project calls for an integrated program in the classical humanities that examines the world of Greco-Roman antiquity through its literature, language, politics, history, philosophy, and art history.

The project's primary aim was to focus on revitalizing and expanding the humanistic tradition by broadening and deepening the scope of existing disciplines in the Associate in Arts and Associate in Science degrees rather than by adding unrelated new courses. At the same time, the program called upon new perspectives in classical research such as the examination of non-Western traditions, social history, and women's studies. With this goal in mind, the College worked toward fostering an historical consciousness and a shared common culture, developing an integrated course of studies, and strengthening a curricular balance at the community college level. It also promoted new links between community college faculty and teachers in local secondary schools. Overall, the project afforded community college students from diverse ethnic, academic, social, and economic backgrounds the opportunity to obtain a balanced education combining rigorous content and practical skills as they studied the ancient texts that underlie the intellectual heritage of Western democracy.

The project was organized so that a common theme, "The Individual and the City in the Ancient World," integrated the disciplines of literature, language, politics, history, philosophy, and art history through the study of specific Greek and Roman classics. Further integration was achieved both laterally and sequentially. For example, during a single semester a Richland student might study the language (Latin), the literature (English 203-The Classical Epic), the history (History 105-The Greeks), and art history (Art History 105-Greek and Roman Art) of antiquity. A student might also move from Humanities 101, a course focusing on the interrelations of classical art, mythology, and philosophy, to Ancient Philosophy 207, the study of Greek and Roman intellectual thought. Another student option might be to move from Latin 101 to Latin 102 or from English 102-Mythology and Writing, a composition course which uses the medium of classical mythology, to the study of the classical epic in English 203.

An additional illustration of how the project works can be seen by examining an introductory American government course now offered at Richland by faculty member Helen Molanphy. Dissatisfied with the materials available, Molanphy developed her own class manual integrating classical literature and culture with information on the American system of government. Students are required to read parts of Plato's *Republic* as well as *Antigone* and *Iphigenia*. In addition, they study the Greek ideal of civic virtue, the classical foundations of the American republic, and classical influences on American art and architecture. Each student is responsible for a final paper connecting a contemporary issue with ancient Greece or Rome. Molanphy has posed such questions as "What did Greek tragedies have to say about war?" and "What were Plato's and Aristotle's ideas about extremes of wealth and poverty?" From the course, says Molanphy, "The students learn, perhaps to their surprise, that there is nothing new under the sun."

The project also provided for in-service opportunities for Richland faculty through a series of intensive, four-week summer seminars held in 1987 and 1988 on the Richland campus. The 1987 summer seminar was entitled "The Individual and the City in the Ancient World." The first week of the seminar focused on the Homeric epic. Classes were led by Professor Karl Galinsky, chair, Department of Classics, University of Texas. Readings included the *Iliad* and the *Odyssey* as well as more modern adaptations of the Ulysses theme in Dante and Tennyson. Week two concentrated on "The Greeks: Cultural, Intellectual, and Political Perspectives," with lectures by Professor Jennifer Roberts, Department of History, Southern Methodist University. Professor Deborah Scott, School of Arts and Humanities, University of Texas, lectured on "Reflections of the City and the Individual in Greek Art" during the third week, with readings from Pollitt's *Art and Experience* and *Art in the Hellenistic Age* as well as a discussion on integrating the classical materials into courses taught by the seminar's participants. The final week of the seminar was devoted to Greek tragedy. Required readings included a number of plays (*Antigone, Oedipus Rex, The Eumenides, Agamemnon, Iphigenia in Taurus*) and critical essays. As usual, time was set aside for discussions of the ways in which participants might integrate the materials into their own courses.

In summer 1988 the classics seminars were devoted to ancient Rome. Participants read and discussed Virgil, Ovid, Plautus, Terence, Horace, Juvenal, and Petronius. In addition, they covered Etruscan art and architecture, Roman painting, the origin, meaning, and functions of satire, and other cultural, intellectual, and political perspectives on the period.

Meanwhile, in the spring and fall of 1987, as part of the Richland "College Classics Cluster Project," a lecture series, "Human Perspectives: From Ancient to Modern," was presented on the campus. Again, scholars from local universities and learning institutions brought their expertise to bear on ways to bridge the gap between classical issues and contemporary concerns as they covered such topics as "Dimensions of the Hero: Past and Present" and "Greek Athletics: Old and New Viewpoints," an examination of the significance of some ancient but remarkably modern criticisms of athletics. The lectures were well attended not only by Richland faculty members and students but also by teachers from area schools and members of the community at large.

Many benefits have accrued from the project, among them the following:

- the interconnections established between the disciplines have encouraged the development of breadth as well as depth; furthermore, these interconnections have enabled faculty to feel renewed by the interdisciplinary exchange and by the team teaching and team planning approaches required for the success of the project;
- the program has given students a historical basis as well as an intercultural perspective for understanding our own and other traditions; it has demonstrated that past traditions influence the present and that there are ancient foundations or prototypes for some of our modern dilemmas;

- the program strengthens the College's academic transfer curriculum by better preparing students for eventual transfer to four-year institutions;
- the lecture series especially promoted new links between teachers at Richland and local secondary schools as well as with scholars and students at nearby four-year colleges and universities.

In conclusion, former project director Nanette Pascal offers the reminder that a particular asset of the program is its applicability to a variety of academic settings. No new courses have been created and no new faculty hired. Instead, professors agreed to expand the courses they were already teaching to include the classics. This approach, according to Pascal, "is the glue that holds together the courses. . .The concept behind the 'Classics Cluster' is not to wait for the students to come to us, but to go where they are. All the students have to take these courses, no matter what their majors may be."

The following is a sampling of Richland College's "Classics Cluster" offerings

English 102—Mythology and Writing

The focus of this course is on developing writing and research skills within the context of classical mythology. Using primary texts in translation, students will read and write about the many dimensions of the classical myths.

Primary Texts: Hesiod, *Theogony*
The *Homeric Hymns*
Selected Greek Dramas
Ovid, *Metamorphoses*

English 203—The Epic

This course explores the epic tradition and its development. The concept of the hero and the interaction of epic heroes within their communities, as viewed in the *Iliad,* the *Odyssey,* and the *Aeneid,* will be analyzed.

Primary Texts: *The Epic of Gilgamesh*
Homer, The *Iliad*
Homer, The *Odyssey*
Vergil, The *Aeneid*

Humanities 101—Our Greek and Roman Heritage

This course analyzes the interrelationships of art, architecture, literature, mythology, and philosophy in the Greco-Roman world. Students will explore essential Greek and Roman ideas and motifs through a comparative approach to ancient sources and contemporary adaptations.

Primary Texts: Plato, *The Trial and Death of Socrates*
Sophocles, *The Tragedies*
Vergil, The *Aeneid*

Government 201—American Government

American Government 201 is a discussion course which concerns the classical roots of the American political system. By examining our Greek and Roman heritage, we gain a better understanding of the current state and future directions of the American political system.

Primary Texts: Plato, *The Republic*
Aristotle, *Politics*
Cicero, Selected Political Speeches
Tacitus, The *Annals* of Imperial Rome

Utah Valley Community College
Orem, Utah

Utah Valley Community College is a two-year college located in Utah County, the second most populous county in the state and one of the fastest growing areas in the nation. Since 1977, the Department of Humanities has experienced a 422 percent enrollment growth; the Division of General Studies, to which the Department of Humanities belongs, has increased from 739 students in 1980 to 3,800 in 1989. The humanities make up one-third of the Division of General Studies. Overall enrollment at the College has increased from 2,000 in 1977 to over 8,000 in 1990, with a projected cap at about 15,000. Approximately one-half of the students are enrolled in Associate in Arts, Associate in Science, or transfer programs.

The majority of the student body comes from Utah, seventy-eight percent from Utah County. In general, students come from communities with relatively small populations and a homogeneous culture. Consequently, the College feels the need to provide its students with a broader insight into the world, past and present.

Under the direction of Elaine Englehardt, the College developed its "Fostering Coherence Through the Humanities" program. The program includes a five-credit-hour humanities core course and a surrounding humanities program consisting of quarterly visits to the College by a nationally known humanities scholar who meets formally and informally with both students and faculty. In addition, a scholar in residence meets for two weeks each summer with humanities faculty. The library's holdings in the humanities have been increased, and the community is invited to participate in lectures and library use.

The humanities core course, required for the Associate in Arts and Associate in Science degrees, is an interdisciplinary ethics and values course in which students explore the disciplines of history, religion, literature, and philosophy through the vehicle of ethics. Students study the foundations of our ethical system and apply them to discussions of such contemporary issues as abortion, euthanasia, business practices, capital punishment, nuclear arms, and sexual relations.

Required texts for the course are *Ethics* by Robert Solomon, *Applying Ethics* by Jeffrey Olen and Vincent Barry, the Bible, "The Death of Ivan Ilyich" by Leo Tolstoy, and *Children of Hiroshima* edited by Arata Osada. Students read selections from the philosophy of Aristotle, Thomas Hobbes, Immanuel Kant, and John Stuart Mill. They interpret ethics through literature by Robert Louis Stevenson, Joseph Conrad, and Feodor Dostoevsky. They examine history through the Constitution, the Declaration of Independence, and *The Federalist Papers*. In addition to the Bible, religion is examined through the Koran and the works of Thomas Aquinas. Thus, the course engages the student in serious reflection of values and ethics inherent in important issues of past and present and how these relate to the student's life.

Faculty development has been a major part of Utah Valley's humanities project through a series of intensive two-week summer courses on ethics. Utah State University has awarded four hours of graduate-level quarter credit for completion of the seminar. In summer 1987, Phyllis Woloshin, professor of philosophy, Oakton Community College, Chicago, conducted a seminar on the fundamentals of ethics and some practical ethics. The summer 1988 seminar was led by Terry Perlin, professor of interdisciplinary studies, Miami University, Ohio, who focused on the history of thought, philosophical concepts, and several practical ethics discussions on medical and legal ethics. In summer 1989 John Woodcock, professor of literature, Indiana University, examined the ethical implications of a number of novels and short stories. The following summer, the College sponsored Dr. Leslie Francis, who centered her workshop on ethics theories of classical philosophers.

Perhaps the effects of Utah Valley Community College's "Fostering Coherence Through the Humanities" project can best be measured by the response of students of this commuter institution, when told by their "Ethics and Values" teacher that they would be required to meet weekly off-campus in addition to their regular meetings, at a place of their own choosing, and without benefit of an instructor. At first, students complained and offered a variety of excuses. But their teacher insisted, and early in the semester each student found a way to attend the out-of-class meetings. In fact, it was suggested by some that once a week was insufficient to cover all the issues.

Humanities faculty and students have benefitted enormously from the humanities project. When asked how she might change the program now that it has been effect for some time, Elaine Englehardt responded, "Honestly, not at all. It has gone smoothly. It has been a tremendous boon to the College, faculty, students, administration, and community."

She added, "Faculty unity is very important. We discussed this program for two years before we implemented it. It was important to share the development of this new program with others, and it was invaluable to bring in their new ideas, explanations, and theories. We have grown with the help of our scholars."

In fact, UVCC faculty and administration were so stimulated by their humanities project and by the opportunities it afforded to meet with colleagues from other institutions that they organized a two-day "Western States Humanities Conference" in October 1989, at the College. Participants had the opportunity to hear an address by Judith Jeffrey Howard, NEH Program Officer, as well as to share with one another information about progress of the humanities in general and specific humanities programs on community college and university campuses throughout the area.

Since then they have developed a two-semester history of civilization course, with Eden Naby, Harvard University, as scholar-in-residence. In conjunction with the course, Naby conducted a seminar for faculty which was an interdisciplinary study of the Middle East.

President Kerry D. Romesburg has articulated well the effects of the College's efforts to advance the humanities: "The establishment of the humanities core program at UVCC, made possible by the strong support of NEH, has been one of the most exciting developments our College has experienced. It provides our students with the traditional foundation for study of the great minds throughout history, and it challenges them to assess and reassess their personal values and ethics within the context of today. We can think of no better way to prepare our students for the challenges of the modern society and workplace."

The following is an excerpt from Utah Valley's "Ethics and Values" course description

Ethics and Values
This is a one-semester, three-credit-hour humanities core course. In addition to the text, professionals from the college and community will lecture and discuss ethics and values under various topic headings. After the student comprehends the issues, three position papers of 3–6 pages will be submitted to the instructors. An invaluable portion of critical thinking is the writing of analytical thoughts in a precise, cohesive, unified form. Students can compare, contrast, and analyze authors, works, ideas, and dogmas in these essays.

Required Reading

From *Great Traditions in Ethics:*

Plato, *Knowledge and Virtue,* Selections from the *Gorgias*

Aristotle, *Moral Character,* Selections from the *Nichomachean Ethics,* Bks. i-ii, vi, x

Thomas Hobbes, *Social Contract Ethics,* Selections from the *Leviathan,* Chapters vi, xiii-xv, xxix-xxx, and *Philosophical Rudiments,* Chapter i

Immanuel Kant, *Duty and Reason,* Selections from *Fundamental Principles of the Metaphysics of Morals,* first and second sections

John Stuart Mill, *The Greatest Happiness Principle,* Selections from *Utilitarianism,* Chapters ii-iii

Carol Gilligan, *In a Different Voice*

Robert Solomon, *Ethics*

Jeffrey Olen and Vincent Barry, *Applying Ethics*

The Bible, any version

Leo Tolstoy, "The Death of Ivan Ilyich"

Henrik Ibsen, *Ghosts*

Alexander Solzhenitsyn, *One Day in the Life of Ivan Denisovich*

Part V
ADVANCING THE HUMANITIES AT TWENTY-FIVE COMMUNITY COLLEGES: EARLY PROGRESS

DESCRIBED BELOW ARE A SAMPLING OF THE ACCOM-plishments of the participating colleges in this year's *Advancing the Humanities* project. The activities demonstrate a broad and creative range of strategies for making the humanities a vital part of the educational lives of students as well as a valuable source of intellectual renewal and satisfaction for faculty.

Adirondack Community College
Glens Falls, New York

For some time, faculty at Adirondack Community College had been concerned about their students' lack of exposure to the humanities. With a humanities curriculum consisting of English, foreign languages, art, music, theater, and philosophy, the College required that candidates for the Associate in Arts degree fulfill a twelve-credit humanities requirement. While Associate in Science degree candidates fulfilled a three-credit requirement, Associate in Applied Science degree candidates, with the exception of those in media arts, had no humanities requirement at all.

To rectify the situation, the College convened a general education committee to discuss the formulation of a humanities core program which would provide students with the necessary tools for future lifelong learning. A core program was designed to meet the following needs:

(1) the development of modes of inquiry, abstract thinking, and critical analysis;
(2) literacy;
(3) the ability to handle quantitative information;
(4) historical consciousness;
(5) exposure to science, art, and international and multicultural experiences;
(6) the study of values formation;
(7) an in-depth study integrating this intellectual development.

Through its involvement in the *Advancing the Humanities* project, and with the valuable assistance of mentor Evelyn Edson, Adirondack Community College has established a humanities core program which is now under way with an enrollment of forty students in two sections. Both faculty and students are pleased with the program: reports are that students are extremely conscious of being in a special group and appreciate the reinforcement the courses give one another. Said one student, "We heard the word *anthropomorphic* three times today—I guess we're going to remember it!" The College hopes to offer summer seminars for faculty to prepare them to teach the interdisciplinary humanities courses planned for the second year of the program. Faculty and administrators involved in the program would like to see greater numbers of their colleagues participate so that they too, as one enthusiastically puts it, "thereby experience the same renewal and rededication to undergraduate education that those of us currently involved now sincerely feel."

Allen County Community College
Iola, Kansas

The present humanities program at Allen County Community College is a diverse one, including a variety of literature, art, music, philosophy, comparative religions, and language courses. However, the College offers neither a core course, interdisciplinary humanities courses, nor courses that address the humanities in relation to technology for career education and occupational certificate program students. With an increasing number of non-traditional students on the campus, faculty and administrators needed to provide two new interdisciplinary courses in the humanities: one for the transfer, liberal arts students in the Associate in Arts degree programs, and one addressing the humanities' relevance to career education students' needs in the business work force, to be incorporated into the Associate in Science degree and certificate programs. In addition, the College wished to establish an advisory council of area business and professional people as well as a program of activities geared to faculty development in the humanities to provide a basis for teaching the courses.

Humanities project leaders along with mentors Joe Collins and Bob Sessions have been working with the College's administrators as they focus on improving their humanities program. Consideration has been given to releasing involved faculty from some teaching duties to prepare adequately for the new interdisciplinary humanities course planned for the spring of 1991. Project directors are focusing their efforts on final syllabus construction, text book selections, campus publicity, and a completed teaching schedule for the instructors involved. Says Sessions, "I believe Allen County's humanities faculty have learned and grown from their efforts. They have an improved understanding of the humanities, of team teaching, and of interdisciplinary courses. Furthermore, they have begun to talk and work with each other in new and constructive ways."

Berkshire Community College
Pittsfield, Massachusetts

In the fall semester of 1989, Berkshire offered 149 humanities courses, maintained in four separate departments. However, a three-credit introduction to the humanities course had not been offered for four years. Meanwhile, the state of Massachusetts had mandated that a core curriculum for both the Associate in Arts and the Associate in Science degrees be established. Thus, the College was faced with the challenge of developing a core humanities offering that would be fresh, engaging, and relevant to all students, whether they were occupational or transfer oriented.

Berkshire Community College *Advancing the Humanities* team members, with the support of mentor Rhonda Kekke, have formulated plans for a revived and revised introduction to the humanities course, focused on the theme of "freedom." The course will be piloted and evaluated in the fall of 1991, with the following goals in mind:

(1) students should learn to develop a higher order of thinking— to learn to see that two contradictory points of view can be defended successfully and that the "truth" often depends on one's perspective;
(2) students should address the question: How can I live successfully and fully as a person and not just as a worker?
(3) students should develop critical thinking skills and develop strategies for thinking about problems;
(4) students should learn to express themselves clearly and persuasively in writing.

Of her site visit to Berkshire, mentor Kekke observed: "The greatest value of this visit, to me, seemed to be how quickly people became excited about the project. Development of a new course should be like one crucial leg of a journey; often, however, if there's no 'grass roots' understanding of the course, it often becomes nothing more than an interesting little side trip. It doesn't last long, is not repeated, and in time is only vaguely remembered even by those who travelled it. I have higher hopes for the Berkshire Community College *Advancing the Humanities* project."

Blue Ridge Community College
Weyers Cave, Virginia

The humanities program at Blue Ridge Community College offered a number of basic survey courses for satisfying the requirements in the humanities for the college-transfer program and for the two-year occupational/technical programs. However, the humanities courses did not always satisfy the needs of highly motivated younger students with some background in the course materials or those of the many older students enjoying the pleasure of continuing their education by exploring the humanities. The College attempted to address these concerns with the establishment of an honors program, a cultural-affairs committee, and an adult degree program in coordination with nearby Mary Baldwin College. Specifically, through participation in the *Advancing the Humanities* project, Blue Ridge Community College received mentor feedback on their new Western and Asian civilization courses and suggestions for improving their first one-credit interdisciplinary honors seminar, as well as an evaluation of the College library humanities holdings.

A team-taught humanities course was put into place in the fall of 1990. The course covers the period from the beginnings of Western literature and philosophy through the Renaissance and is conducted as a seminar, with discussion and independent learning projects. In addition, a three-block course with the common theme "Ways of Knowing" has been prepared. It requires students to enroll simultaneously in three linked classes: composition, introduction to psychology, and Western civilization. The block course will be team taught. Plans are under way to offer these courses in the spring. For the future, the humanities team plans to develop articulation agreements for new and existing courses with James Madison University and Mary Baldwin College. The agreements are expected to help enrollment in the honors program courses.

Blue Ridge *Advancing the Humanities* project members are enthusiastic in their praise of their mentor, Agnes Pollock: "AACJC's selection of Jefferson State as a mentor college was an excellent choice, since Jefferson State, with assistance from AACJC and NEH, has produced a series of exemplary humanities courses for their honors program and instituted a very impressive faculty development seminar series in the humanities . . . we learned a lot from our visit to Jefferson State, and we look forward to continuing our very fruitful association with that college and our mentor."

Cabrillo College
Aptos, California

Although Cabrillo College offered over one hundred humanities courses in its catalog when it applied for participation in the *Advancing the Humanities* project, the College humanities offerings lacked coherence. No formal attempt had been made to integrate studies; thus students learned each humanities subject in isolation and had to find the connections among them on their own. The approach to the selection of humanities courses did not foster the study of the humanities in sequence or generate breadth of knowledge. Furthermore, ethnic minority student enrollment had increased by sixty percent from 1985 to 1989. Thus, more humanities courses were needed to lead the way to the development of appreciation and understanding of other cultures and to provide the opportunity for the exploration of non-Western cultures in relationship to Western tradition.

To those ends, Cabrillo College has designed a model one-year humanities curriculum that answers the need for breadth, sequence, and coherence. Through the reading of original texts, students are engaged in the study of both Western and non-Western cultural traditions through the following course sequence:

Fall 1990—Western Civilization I, English Composition, Philosophy;

Spring 1991—Non-Western Philosophy, English Composition and Literature, Art History.

In addition, at a series of meetings and workshops, faculty are reviewing issues in humanities instruction and the development of a coherent humanities program to focus college-wide attention on solving the problem areas.

According to mentor Barbara Morgridge after her site visit: "It was apparent in talking with the instructors that they have already begun to eye further possibilities for instruction as they work with and respond to their bright, capable students and that, as they become more conversant and comfortable with cooperative learning strategies, as well as other means of student-teacher interaction in coordinated studies, they will refine the shape and content of their humanities program . . . All in all, the project is well and securely launched and the group's efforts to advance the humanities at Cabrillo are both inspiring and, at times, inspired . . . In view of their well-prepared and organized approach to the first phase of their project, it appears certain that they will complete their entire project as planned."

Central Florida Community College
Ocala, Florida

When Central Florida Community College was offered the opportunity to participate in the *Advancing the Humanities* project, it was faced with a number of formidable challenges: a dramatic enrollment in humanities classes because the College serves the nation's second-fastest growing metropolitan area; the merging of the English and history departments; and the recent acquisition by the College of the Appleton Museum, including its major collections of African and Asian art as well as important holdings in Western art. In response to these challenges, Central Florida sought to strengthen the required freshman humanities course and to coordinate the other humanities courses into a more coherent sequence. In addition, the College wished to develop and implement classes in the non-Western humanities to take advantage of the Appleton Museum holdings.

Following the AACJC/NEH National Humanities Conference and with the advice and support of mentor Agnes Pollock, the Central Florida team has effected a number of important changes, among them the following:

(1) transforming the one-semester introduction to humanities course into a two-semester sequence, thus offering students an in-depth introduction to the humanities;

(2) initiating a study to explore the connections between the new six-hour humanities sequence and the six-hour world history sequence that covers the same time period; a preliminary curriculum has already been presented at the fall meeting of the southern division of the Community College Humanities Association;

(3) planning the implementation of a trial program consisting of a twelve-hour humanities and world history sequence that will be team taught, that will use primary sources, and that will use an integrated and interdisciplinary approach to delineate the main elements of humanities and history.

Of their mentor, team members report: "Agnes Pollock was able to give concrete advice on how to involve faculty, design a program, and secure funding. . . In summary, Ms. Pollock gave Central Florida Community College information on how to pursue its own aims as well as provide us with sources of inspiration and warning."

Chemeketa Community College
Salem, Oregon

Chemeketa Community College began as a vocational/technical institution, but has grown into a comprehensive institution which provides college transfer, lifelong learning, and developmental skill-building classes as well. The College has a humanities program which offers courses in speech, philosophy, religion, foreign languages, music, theater, English, art, film, and communications. Its faculty is academically strong and diverse. However, Chemeketa was faced with a central problem: should the humanities department act simply as a provider of general education courses, or should it be an educational leader by developing strategies for providing students with new ways of learning and establishing interdisciplinary humanities linkages? Eager to accept the challenge, Chemeketa's humanities faculty developed a plan for advancing the humanities which consisted of a multidisciplinary block course entitled "The Evolving American Culture." The new nine-credit course merges three disciplines: literature, history, and film studies; it meets students' requirements for sequence in an elective, social science, and the humanities.

Through participation in the *Advancing the Humanities* project, Chemeketa team members were provided with valuable insights from mentors as well as from colleagues at other colleges who have undertaken similar initiatives. They received support from mentor Kathy Fedorko, who was especially helpful in bringing a new perspective to the development of the block course. She directed the team away from male-centered language and gave specific suggestions for women's writing. They have developed a marketing brochure for the block course and worked with the College's counseling staff as well as area high schools to recruit students. Over the past year they have convinced the administration of the benefits of the interdisciplinary humanities course and have received the financing and release time for summer planning and designing as well as for supporting full implementation. They have also given presentations on the course at faculty in-service meetings, at the CCHA Pacific Northwestern Conference in conjunction with Saddleback College, an *Advancing the Humanities* Year One college, and at the Pacific Northwest Conference on Teaching English.

Delighted with the fruits of their labors, team members are devising ways to develop a faculty renewal project and have visited Prince George's Community College to observe a model program at work. They see great possibilities in exploring combinations of cross disciplines directed toward a faculty program to erode curricular barriers and benefit faculty as well as students.

The following is a list of films accompanying "The Evolving American Culture," Chemeketa Community College's three-course block of linked disciplines

First Theme: Roaring 20's and Depressing 30's

Week I March 27–29
Elmer Gantry (Richard Brooks, 1960), Academy Award to Burt Lancaster

Week II April 1–5
Mr. Deeds Goes to Town (Frank Capra, 1935), crazy comedy with Gary Cooper and Jean Arthur

Week III April 8–12
The Grapes of Wrath (John Ford, 1940), two Academy Awards, Henry Fonda classic

Second Theme: Violence in America

Week IV April 15–19
Public Enemy (William Wellman, 1931), a Cagney classic

Week V April 22–26
Dr. Strangelove (Stanley Kubrick, 1964), Peter Sellers playing multiple roles

Third Theme: Men and Women

Week VI April 29–May 3
To Have and Have Not (Howard Hawks, 1944), Bogart/Bacall classic

Week VII May 6–10
Adam's Rib (George Cukor, 1949), Spencer Tracy/Katharine Hepburn

Fourth Theme: The Individual and Society

Week VIII May 13–17
Rebel Without a Cause (Nicholas Ray, 1955), James Dean/Natalie Wood

Week IX May 20–24
Invasion of the Body Snatchers (Don Siegel, 1956), the original

Week X May 27–31
Bonnie and Clyde (Arthur Penn, 1967), Warren Beatty, Faye Dunaway and Gene Hackman (his first film), a sixties classic

Part V

Clark State Community College
Springfield, Ohio

On the strength of its existing humanities program, in July 1988 Clark Technical College was granted its request by the Ohio Board of Regents to become Clark State Community College. Clark State had already developed a strong humanities program in the study of the Western world; now it recognized the need to internationalize the curriculum. It also recognized the connection between reading great books and understanding culture and values. Consequently, Clark State developed a two-pronged plan: to expose both technical and non-technical faculty to non-Western cultures, especially through the study of the great books of those cultures, and to develop coursework in the humanities reflecting this exposure. The large influx of Japanese corporations in the region has led to a decision to begin with the study of East Asia.

Thus far, Clark State has taken a number of important steps toward the completion of its project: four major scholars have agreed to become part of the program; the Japan Society, the Japan Foundation, and the National Clearinghouse for Japanese Studies at Indiana University have offered assistance; and the College has received an NEH grant to hold community lectures on Japanese culture, a series of faculty seminars, and regional studies courses for transfer and career students modelled on the "Other Civilizations" concept proposed in *50 Hours: A Core Curriculum for College Students* by NEH Chair Lynne Cheney. One-third of the Clark State faculty will take part in a 1991 Summer Institute on Japanese Culture. Reported enthusiastic mentor Isa Engleberg after her visit to Clark State, "This humanities team is right on target."

Community College of Allegheny County, South Campus
West Mifflin, Pennsylvania

Although the Community College of Allegheny County, South Campus offers a number of humanities courses, there has been no formal attempt to coordinate the content of these courses. Furthermore, the majority of students who elect these courses are in transfer programs, while vocational/technical students often take only one humanities course as part of the general distribution requirements of the Associ-

58

Community College of Allegheny County-South Campus promotes Humanities Week at the College.

ate in Arts or Associate in Science degree. Nonetheless, to be successful human beings as well as successful wage earners in a region that now houses the corporate headquarters of multi-national corporations, students need an introduction to the values, ethics, thinking and standards that are developed through the humanities.

To serve these students as well as a faculty that must adopt teaching styles and methods to accommodate career-minded students who often combine family responsibilities, work, and academic pursuits, the South Campus of the Community College of Allegheny County proposed a humanities project focusing upon the wealth of regional art, music, history, and literature. Through the project, the College hoped to increase faculty awareness of the vast resources in the region that could be used to broaden student perspectives of themselves, the region, the nation, and the world; create student awareness of the humanities; and outline a tentative course that can be integrated into the curriculum.

Thus far, with the advice of mentors Karen Bojar and Grace Flisser, humanities team members have written a three-part proposal which has been approved and funded by the administration. The project offers a small stipend to instructors to include a humanities-based component in their courses, to describe it in detail in writing, to present it to other faculty members, and to conduct a follow-up evaluation. Nine faculty members are now working on the *Advancing the Humanities* project. They have sponsored a number of lectures by renowned scholars on interdisciplinary concerns. The group planned a variety of activities for Humanities Week, November 11–16, 1990, among them a showing of Spike Lee's *Do the Right Thing*, along with ethical and philosophical reading materials and discussion; an arts and lights production; and a slide-tape show of a business ethics teacher's travels in Wyoming, with a voice-over narration that presents historical and cultural perspectives.

Team members report that their work has already produced change at the College. Says one member of the faculty, "Interest has been raised not only within the English department and the humanities disciplines, but outside as well. The project has served to pull a revitalized faculty together in a shared project wherein they are developing new areas of scholarship and working to share interests with each other and with their students."

Eastern Wyoming College
Torrington, Wyoming

Humanities courses at Eastern Wyoming College are, for the most part, distributed among a number of departments: English, art, history, music, communication, and theater. Furthermore, the College does not have a humanities requirement, so that enrollment for humanities courses is generally low. Humanities team members from Eastern Wyoming hope to strengthen humanities requirements at the College and to encourage wider appreciation of the value of studying the humanities. Currently, with the support of mentor Elaine Englehardt, they are involved in a number of activities designed to help them and the College reach the goals they have set for themselves.

Thus far, the team has presented a plan for a faculty development seminar to the faculty at large. In addition, they have proposed a humanities-centered lecture series to which all faculty would be invited. Mentor Englehardt met with the College's new president, Roy Mason, who expressed a strong commitment to and approval of the program. In addition, she met with other senior administrators to reinforce their enthusiasm for adding a humanities course to the College degree requirements. A long-range goal of the team is to implement a core course in the humanities as well as to require an additional humanities course for the distribution course requirements. The humanities faculty is also committed to building alliances with the trade, vocational, business, and industrial faculty. Through these alliances, it is hoped that more humanities concepts will be taught in courses outside the humanities.

Says mentor Englehardt: "It was fun and exciting to work with the dedicated faculty and administration at Eastern Wyoming College; they have a strong commitment to the advancement of the humanities. . .I'm sure the *Advancing the Humanities* project will have a profound effect on the students, faculty, administration, and community."

Elgin Community College
Elgin, Illinois

Although Elgin Community College has been offering a full range of humanities offerings for some time, none of the courses has a prerequisite, and only one is team taught. The College humanities team felt that the current humanities curriculum lacked a central, cohesive focus. They believed that students would benefit from a team-taught, interdisciplinary course which would involve instructors from various humanities disciplines. With the assistance of mentor Rhonda Kekke, team members have helped to strengthen the humanities curriculum at the College.

Summer and fall release time was granted to four faculty members so that they were able to design a pilot humanities course projected for the spring of 1991, while the College humanities requirement has been increased from three to nine credits. In addition, the College will act as host for the 1992 Central Division Community College Humanities Association meeting. It presented its own progress report at the 1990 CCHA regional meeting in Rockford, Illinois.

Site visits between team members and mentor Kekke have been mutually beneficial. In fact, said Kekke, "At times, during my visit

*Team members
Donna Wojcik,
RayLene Corgiat,
and Margie
Williams
(second, fourth,
and fifth from
left) meet with
other Genesee
Community
College faculty
members to plan
a new humanities
course.*

to Elgin, I found myself having a slight bit of trouble remembering what I was there to advance! . . . We discovered that our two colleges are good 'mutual mentors' in many areas . . . I even brought back some good ideas gleaned from Elgin's college catalog!"

Genesee Community College
Batavia, New York

Although Genesee Community College offers a variety of humanities course offerings, for many students and faculty members a humanities course is a low priority in program schedules already burdened with many credit hours devoted to technical training. Through participation in the *Advancing the Humanities* project, the College has been able to work toward meeting three long-range goals:

(1) increased acceptance by all faculty of the need for humanities study;
(2) development of humanities courses specifically focused on the needs of career students;
(3) implementation of a general education requirement of at least one humanities course for all matriculating career program students.

Toward those ends, team members organized a fall faculty humanities seminar. Edwin Delattre, Olin Scholar in Applied Ethics, Boston University, addressed the entire faculty on the importance of the humanities to education. He also led a targeted group of five career education and five humanities faculty members through a discussion of a specific humanities text and its application to the world of work. The College is planning a faculty summer institute with the hope that it will lead to the development of new interdisciplinary courses.

In addition to valuable assistance from mentors Karen Bojar and Grace Flisser, the team has benefited from the insights of Bob Sessions and Joe Collins, Kirkwood Community College, whose project closely models one Genesee Community College would like to develop. Team members, enthusiastic after their visit to Kirkwood, reported, "We shared our ideas with Bob Sessions, Joe Collins, and others, and received a great deal of good feedback and advice."

Hawaii Community College
Hilo, Hawaii

Hawaii Community College is unique in that it functions as one unit within the University of Hawaii. Sharing a campus with the University as it does, for the most part the College has geared its curriculum toward skill development rather than broader questions dealing with the humanities perspectives. Recently, however, a pilot program consisting of interdisciplinary, team-taught courses focused around a common theme was pioneered at Hawaii Community College. In an attempt to build on the progress already made in "humanitizing the curriculum," the College *Advancing the Humanities* team has set for its goal the planning and implementation of two new courses. With the able assistance of mentor Barbara Morgridge, the team has also learned the necessity for faculty development and has explored ways to develop faculty support to help meet its goals.

The first of the projected courses is a multicultural literature course that can be taught from a variety of different perspectives: international ethnic groups, various American ethnics, or the works of Asian American women, for example. The second course is a revision of a present reading course to focus on reading and rhetorical skills to aid in the development of critical thinking. The course, through the analysis of short stories, great literary works, and essays, studied from a multidisciplinary perspective, will add meaningful humanities content to an essentially skills-oriented course.

A site visit by mentor Morgridge provided useful and concrete assistance to team members through syllabus suggestions, the exploration of strategies for interesting other faculty in the multicultural course, and the distribution of a film catalog. After a visit to their mentor campus, team members began to consider the possibility of including English as a Second Language (ESL) students in their new course enrollment. They believe that their participation in the *Advancing the Humanities* project will help the students broaden their values and beliefs as they develop an understanding of and an appreciation for the humanities.

Iowa Central Community College
Fort Dodge, Iowa

Although degree students at Iowa Central Community College have had a humanities requirement (eight hours for the Associate in Arts, four hours for the Associate in Science), vocational/technical students have been required to take only the minimum general education courses possible, and these courses do not have a humanities basis. Thus, these students are not exposed to an overview of all the humanities and their interrelationships. Iowa Central *Advancing the Humanities* team members have embarked upon a program to develop a humanities curriculum accessible to all students. In addition, they are working on promoting a positive attitude toward the humanities by all staff members of the College through a staff development program.

Working with assigned mentor Lee Paez in addition to receiving valuable input from Bob Sessions, Iowa Central's team conducted a one-day workshop to examine the areas of work and play through the humanities. This was the institution's first retreat and it was rated well by participants (4.55 out of a 5-point scale). According to Paez, humanities team members saw the retreat "as a pivotal event for building more bridges with the technology faculty and laying the groundwork for significant and positive change." Also in the works is a three-week faculty institute.

Meanwhile, the team and mentor Paez have exchanged site visits which exposed team members to new ways of teaching the humanities and to a variety of programmatic approaches to promoting humanities education. On the Iowa Central campus, Paez, joined by Bob Sessions, was able to meet with college administrators and key humanities and technology faculty. Later that day, she addressed a group of sixty faculty members on the centrality of humanities education and described the model humanities programs at Richland College.

Lake City Community College
Lake City, Florida

The humanities core program at Lake City Community College consists of two courses: one emphasizing art and music, the other philosophy and religion. The two courses are supplemented by a number of optional courses drawn from these same four areas. The faculty has expressed concern over the lack of focus of such a program. Thus, the College humanities team has as its goals a revision of the College curriculum to ensure students a more cohesive exposure to the humanities, specifically through a great books program, and the design and implementation of a faculty development program.

The team has the support of mentor Evelyn Edson, who paid the College a site visit and met with key administrators and faculty. She spoke with them of Piedmont's humanities program and suggested humanities activities which could be pursued at Lake City.

Thus far, team members have called a meeting of liberal arts faculty, the vice-president for instruction, and other interested parties to report on their humanities activities. The team conducted a two-and-one-half-hour all-faculty seminar on the myth of Orpheus and Eurydice, examining the effects of the Black Orpheus legend on modern music. Meanwhile, the team continues to explore a variety of ways in which to bring the great books into the College curriculum. The plan envisions initiating annual faculty discussions on the proposed core of great books. These seminars would cross-train social scientists, historians, other humanists, mathematicians, and scientists to present portions of the great books core curriculum in their own courses.

Lake Michigan College
Benton Harbor, Michigan

Traditionally, humanities education at Lake Michigan College has been offered in a fragmented way. Although many humanities courses are available, for the most part students in the occupational studies programs already have a full load of required non-humanities courses, so that very few are exposed to what the humanities can offer.

Furthermore, these courses are not broad based to include a contextual introduction to the humanities. Finally, there has been a lack of interaction, integration, and coordination of curricula between the humanities offerings and the programs in the occupational studies division.

Thus far, the Lake Michigan College team has devoted its efforts to initiating a dialogue between the humanities and the occupational faculty. They have met with considerable success. Currently, faculty from trades, vocations, technology, social sciences, nursing, and humanities are involved in the project. With their support, the humanities team has formulated a twelve-point plan that integrates the humanities into their classrooms. Says mentor Elaine Englehardt, "The result is impressive. I believe that the twelve educational factors that have been developed by this team could be implemented in courses across the country. I am impressed with the far reaching effects that a project such as this one can have on a college and community."

The team continues to work on ways of incorporating the twelve points into the occupational curricula and is planning a series of faculty workshops and study sessions to that end, with the support of President Anne Mulder and other key College administrators. Adds Englehardt, "President Mulder has expressed a deep commitment to the humanities at Lake Michigan College. She is an exceptional leader and is willing to implement cutting-edge changes that are necessary for the College."

The following are highlights of Lake Michigan College's twelve-point plan for integrating the humanities into the classroom

1. Historical Perspective: Understanding a concept/theory/idea/problem well requires a comprehension of the context in which the idea is presented.
2. Considering the Viewpoints of Others: Being capable of considering the viewpoints of others implies that a person. . .can, with an open mind, consider what others have expressed as their opinion, position, or idea in arriving at solutions and decisions or in making plans.
3. Effective Communication: Effective communicating requires a recognition of particular characteristics. . .to gain personal rapport and an understanding of individual motivators.
4. Critical Thinking: Critical thinking consists of identifying, evaluating and, if necessary, challenging the ideas and underlying assumptions while exploring and imagining alternatives.
5. Problem Solving: Problem solving requires the step-by-step application of specific skills.
6. Decision Making: Making a decision involves the process whereby one of several possible solutions to a particular problem must be selected.
7. Responding to Change—Adaptation: Adaptation refers to appropriate response by an individual to changes within his/her physical, social, and work environment.
8. Clarification of Value Options: Clarification of value options includes the recognition of ethical implications, aesthetic factors, and pragmatic considerations.
9. Civic Purpose and Responsible Citizenship: This refers to an appreciation of the responsibility of each person for civic, consumer, environmental, and social activities that support the common good, both nationally and internationally.
10. Cultural Diversity: Multicultural education is preparation for the social, political, and economic realities that individuals experience in culturally diverse and complex human encounters.
11. Creativity: Creativity is the mental attitude that inspires a willingness to ask questions, and the motivation to explore answers beyond the immediate or obvious.
12. Self-Awareness: Self-awareness involves understanding one's personal and social self.

Massachusetts Bay Community College team members Eleanor Smith and Harold White conduct their new class, Hum. 115, Wisdom for the Workplace.

Massachusetts Bay Community College
Wellesley Hills, Massachusetts

While transfer students at Massachusetts Bay Community College (MBCC) tended to value the humanities as an intrinsic part of their education, career students, seventy-five percent of the student population, frequently saw the humanities as having little or no bearing on their preparation for employment. In fact, humanities courses made few direct connections between value-oriented and theoretical content and the world of work. To bridge the gap, the College humanities team developed a two-pronged plan.

The team created a business advisory board for the College composed of representatives of ten diverse corporations in the Boston area. The board identified five workplace problems involving human relations. These problems were developed into a case studies document and became part of a new team-taught course for business students entitled "Wisdom in the Workplace." In the course, students use critical thinking skills to analyze the cases and study major works of literature to gain insights into specific values. The syllabus consists of fourteen literary works taken from the classical, medieval, and modern periods, including *Antigone, Canterbury Tales,* Benjamin Franklin's *Autobiography,* and Saul Bellow's *Seize the Day.*

Mentor Rhonda Kekke is delighted with the progress the humanities team has made: "The people I visited with at MBCC deserve to feel very proud of their accomplishments . . . What this College has achieved is impressive."

Middlesex Community College
Bedford, Massachusetts

Two campuses, many disciplines in one division, and a number of strong but separate initiatives have led to a lack of community among Middlesex Community College humanities faculty. In addition, the expansion into two permanent campuses has generated a culturally diverse student body whose many traditions offer the opportunity and the motivation for faculty study in comparative approaches to humanities content.

In response to this set of challenges, the Middlesex humanities team developed a plan to offer intellectual development and collegiality to its faculty while working toward helping students to understand and appreciate the cultures of their fellow students and citizens.

The project, entitled "Common Ground," consists of a series of lectures and summer workshops for faculty of both campuses on Latin American literature and Southeast Asian culture. First, team members held a series of small group meetings with Middlesex faculty to describe the plan and elicit support. With financial assistance from the administration, two scholarly lectures were scheduled for the end of the spring semester. The lectures were designed to familiarize the faculty with the topic areas being considered for future study, to focus on intellectual development rather than on pedagogy, to "audition" the lecturers as potential scholars for the summer workshops, and to expose the campus community to the richness of Latin American studies.

Humanities team members were delighted with the opportunity to work with mentor Isa Engleberg, whose own college's exemplary project serves as a valuable model for Middlesex. Reported Engleberg, after a spring visit to the Middlesex campus: "The team members from Middlesex are enthusiastic and inspired! In the short time since the National Humanities Conference, they have accomplished more than some colleges will accomplish in a year. The faculty is well aware of the *Advancing the Humanities* project, understands the action plan, and supports the efforts of the team."

Mississippi Gulf Coast Community College
Gulfport, Mississippi

Mississippi Gulf Coast has offered a number of courses in the humanities over the years, but none of them has focused on relationships between the various disciplines except for an honors colloquium. Thus, only a few, select students have had the opportunity to experience interdisciplinary approaches to the humanities. Participation in the *Advancing the Humanities* project has enabled the College to offer more students this valuable opportunity.

To begin with, the humanities team formed a committee to generate interest in developing interdisciplinary courses in the humanities. Out of approximately twenty fulltime humanities instructors, ten expressed interest in doing so.

In the fall of 1990 the College offered its pilot course, "The World," a team taught offering combining world literature and world history. Plans are afoot to build upon the success of the pilot course by offering the second half of "The World" in the spring semester and by supporting other faculty members' course development.

Mentor Lee Paez made a site visit to the College to advise on the new interdisciplinary course and to meet in small group settings with the College president, Barry L. Mellinger, other key administrators, and interested faculty to discuss and encourage efforts underway to advance the humanities at Mississippi Gulf Coast. Said Paez after her visit, "The project in terms of the success of the pilot course is in very good shape." She encouraged enthusiastic students enrolled in the course to write letters to the board of trustees describing the values they derived from their experience. The course is providing students with the opportunity to explore the interrelationships and interdependence of liberal arts disciplines in the humanities.

Northeast Texas Community College
Mt. Pleasant, Texas

Northeast Texas Community College has had a traditional humanities program consisting of courses in a variety of disciplines: English, art, music, philosophy, and history. However, the College has not offered an integrated humanities course providing students with a world civilization framework. Such an approach is especially needed in a college whose students are frequently first-generation college students and are lacking in basic cultural knowledge in history, literature, philosophy, and the arts. Consequently, the College *Advancing the Humanities* plan involves devising ways to provide an integrated, team teaching approach to teaching the humanities. The team believes that such an approach is necessary when working with students who have many gaps in their base of cultural knowledge.

To implement their plan, the team embarked upon a number of steps, beginning with reviewing existing curricula in the humanities and surveying current student enrollment in the humanities. They then appointed a humanities advisory committee and created a model of their proposed course, a six-hour core offering that would include a cultural-historical overview with specific content in art, music, history, philosophy, and literature and require attendance at performances in the College Art Center.

In addition, the humanities team appointed an interdisciplinary committee to teach the core, with one anchor teacher in all courses and a second teacher or teachers in other disciplines. The plan required the review of scheduling and load impact of such a model as well as presentation to the general faculty for reaction and questions. The course is scheduled for the fall of 1991.

Northern Virginia Community College
Sterling, Virginia

Before their arrival at the *Advancing the Humanities* conference, members of Northern Virginia's humanities team already knew that their humanities course was being planned for the fall semester of 1990. However, members of the teaching team, although highly conversant in their own fields, had never systematically looked at Western culture from the perspective of other humanities disciplines. They needed help in clarifying their syllabus so that appropriate works of enduring value were integrated into the syllabus reading list and treatment of the texts incorporated both recent scholarly interpretations and currently successful pedagogical approaches to great books. They were convinced that the team-building and networking opportunities afforded by participation in the *Advancing the Humanities* project would be invaluable to the team and ultimately to those at the College who would in turn be reached, students and faculty alike.

Unfortunately, early in the fall of 1990, the course was cancelled as a result of a College-wide budget crunch. Nevertheless, team members continue to feel that through their participation in the humanities project they learned a great deal about the design and

David Whipple, assistant professor of art history, right, discusses a new interdisciplinary humanities course with other Northern Virginia Community College humanities team members, left to right, R. Neil Reynolds, provost, Agatha Taormina, professor of English, and Beverly Blois, professor of history.

implementation of a multidisciplinary course. In addition to working with mentor Bernice Kliman, the team made a site visit to Jefferson State to observe team teaching in action and were able to discuss course design and the recruitment and retention of students. They also were provided with course syllabi and suggestions for audio-visual materials.

Mentor Kliman is hopeful that Northern Virginia will be able to implement its planned course at a later date. During her site visit she made some suggestions for adapting the course to a broader segment of the student population. She also had the opportunity to learn about efforts to introduce an international component into all courses at the College. "Speaking to those involved was a wonderful example of the mentor mentored; I gathered materials that I can bring back to my college. We, too, are eager to introduce international elements in many courses, and I see this as a way to advance the humanities."

Pennsylvania College of Technology
Williamsport, Pennsylvania

In July 1989, the Pennsylvania College of Technology, formerly the Williamsport Area Community College, was created to provide vocational and technical education statewide. Affiliated with the Pennsylvania State University, the College sees its expanded role as presenting a challenge and an opportunity to the humanities to remain a vital part of the College's new, expanded educational mission. Although associate degree students are required to take three credits in the humanities or social sciences as part of the general education core, humanities course offerings are generally traditional and primarily discipline focused. Humanities faculty have sought to extend student contact with the humanities through organizing a series of interdisciplinary colloquia designed to demonstrate the relationship of various approaches to knowledge. Nevertheless, the limited course requirement for students presents difficulties for student exposure to the breadth of humanistic concepts as does the discipline-based approach to learning. Furthermore, non-humanities faculty have been reluctant to take release time from the study of career skills to devote to the humanities. Consequently, the College humanities team has set as its goals an increased dialogue between humanities and vocational/ technical faculty, the development of a team-taught interdisciplinary humanities course, and the designing of strategies for stimulating faculty to develop additional interdisciplinary humanities courses and alternative approaches.

The team has been exceptionally active since its attendance at the *Advancing the Humanities* conference. A humanities task force made up of technologies and humanities faculty members has been formed. To create the task force, the team formulated a survey asking for choices of topics for a series of summer seminars and for task force volunteers. The survey yielded thirty-one volunteers, from which eight were chosen. Since then, the task force has been planning a summer 1991 seminar on Native American culture. The two-to-three-day seminar will be led by a member of the English department and will feature guest speakers. In addition, a cross-disciplinary course has been developed by two humanities team members. The course, "The American Woman: Herstory Through Her Literature," will combine an historical and literary approach and will be offered in the spring 1991 semester.

Site visits between team members and mentor Kathy Fedorko have proved helpful and stimulating. During her visit to Pennsylvania College of Technology, Fedorko was able to meet with key administrators and encourage them to continue their support for pilot team teaching and to press for more humanities requirements. Team members also visited Piedmont Virginia Community College to observe its faculty development seminar in action. The response was enthusiastic. "The visit helped by showing that what is now just a possibility on this campus can in fact become not just reality but a stimulating, long-term beneficial activity for a diverse faculty, with valuable impact on students."

Salt Lake Community College
Salt Lake City, Utah

Salt Lake Community College has recently evolved from a purely technical college and is experiencing the growing pains that come from a rapid expansion of the curriculum to accommodate a matching population increase of transfer students. A number of fine arts and humanities courses are available for general education students. However, technical and vocational students still find it difficult to fit humanities courses into their tight schedules, although under new guidelines, all students will be required to take five quarter hours of an interdisciplinary course outside their program. Rapid growth of the College has created an unnecessary division among faculty and students based upon their chosen programs.

Salt Lake's *Advancing the Humanities* team has selected as its goal to bring together the excellent faculties of the College, regardless of their respective disciplines, through the development of an interdisciplinary, team-taught course available to all students entering programs of either career or transfer capabilities. The course will offer an introduction to the arts as well as an exploration of value systems of the past. Taught primarily by a humanities instructor, the course will include modules from various technical programs showing practical connections between the humanities concepts and the personal and occupational worlds of the students. The team is also formulating ideas for the establishment of a steering committee made up of faculty from humanities, business, nursing, technical, and vocational programs. Also in the works is the consideration of a visit from a

Mentor Kathy Fedorko, left, listens as Theresa Crater and Michael Beehler, South Puget Sound Community College, describe their team's humanities plan.

humanities scholar to conduct a seminar/workshop on the design of the interdisciplinary course.

Mentors Joe Collins and Bob Sessions, in light of their own successful experience in bridging the technology/humanities gap, proved to be valuable sources of support and information. Team members came away from site visits with an increased awareness of the importance of devising methods of establishing closer ties among faculty as the first step toward any changes in the curriculum. They saw how valuable the seminar process is and gained appreciation for the groundwork that goes into its successful implementation.

South Puget Sound Community College
Olympia, Washington

In 1988, South Puget Sound Community College was declared a separate community college district. It has recently changed emphasis from a technical college to an institution offering both Associate in Technical Arts and Associate in Arts degrees. In addition, it is now in its third year of an NEH grant to create a coherent and comprehensive humanities program. Humanities team members from South Puget Sound came to the *Advancing the Humanities* conference with the wish to continue developing their humanities program by bringing American literature, non-Western humanities, and coordinated studies into the curriculum. They sought help in devising ways to integrate students' learning through linked courses, cluster courses, and coordinated studies programs as well as in organizing and presenting increasingly broad areas of information for use in a community college program. Also on the agenda was the development of strategies to deal with administrative problems associated with changing teaching approaches.

A series of meetings of the humanities department have been held to create more coherence in the curriculum. Discussion within the faculty has been stimulating and has resulted in the creation of a seminar linking courses covering the classical period.

A site visit by mentor Kathy Fedorko generated increased support for the project among key campus leaders with whom she met. In addition, she was able to offer valuable suggestions after attending a humanities department meeting. The team also visited the Kirkwood campus to meet with Robert Sessions and Joseph Collins and observe their program integrating humanities with the occupational curriculum. Reported Collins, "The primary value of the visit was that it allowed the Puget Sound team to see exactly what our project is all about. They can use this as a sample framework on which they can formulate their own ideas."

Team members said of their visit, "We were strongly encouraged by Kirkwood's example to build on our history as a technological college and bring our humanities dialogue to the whole faculty. We can anticipate a give and take process, whereby humanities faculty not only share the importance of humanities in the Associate in Technical Arts program but can be encouraged themselves to better understand technology issues and how they affect our culture."

Thomas Nelson Community College
Hampton, Virginia

Although Thomas Nelson Community College (TNCC) offers humanities courses which are individually strong, they do not add up to a fully articulated program. A recent mission task force cited the need for a strong, general education component in both technical and college transfer curricula. In response to this need, the College humanities team has called for an integration of the humanities into the entire College curriculum rather than an increase of distribution requirements and the development of new survey courses. With the aid of mentor Bernice Kliman, the team has devised a number of ways to generate awareness of and interest in the humanities for both faculty and students.

Thus far, the College has made considerable progress toward its goal of focusing on activities that complement classroom learning. A recently established cultural affairs committee hosted a one-person Mark Twain performance drawing upon the full spectrum of Twain's writings. A professional actor, Ken Richters, used thirty excerpts from Twain's speeches, private notes, books, plays, and essays to bring students into contact with the best of Twain's thought. The committee is engaged in making contact with a number of other sources of talent to arrange for future programs. In addition, they are coordinating their efforts with student activities programs and planning ongoing faculty/staff/students activities such as film/discussion series and great books discussions.

The team is also turning their attention to faculty development, particularly as it impinges on introducing critical thinking into all classes offered at the College. Mentor Kliman is assisting the team as they design a faculty development initiative on this topic, starting with written goals and progressing to the design of class sessions that enhance critical thinking for specific disciplines.

A full range of activities was planned for team members during their site visit to their mentor college. After attending a faculty seminar at Nassau Community College, one team member noted: "Nassau is proof that an 'aging faculty' can be remotivated. My visit made me return to TNCC with ideas to share with my colleague who is involved in the critical thinking part of our *Advancing the Humanities* project. It made me realize how lucky we were to receive an award that gives us and those we mentor the release time to revamp our curricula. To sum up, Dr. Kliman did a remarkable job, and I feel that every person I met and every activity in which I took part was well planned and relevant to Thomas Nelson Community College's *Advancing the Humanities* strategy."

Part VI

ADVANCING THE HUMANITIES AT TWENTY-FOUR COMMUNITY COLLEGES: THE COMMITMENT CONTINUES

"The Advancing the Humanities *project has provided our College with a broad perspective of the humanities movement throughout the United States. This program has enabled us to learn from the successes of the model programs and to apply fresh ideas to our humanities program."*

Roy Church, president
Lorain County Community College

TWENTY-FOUR COMMUNITY, TECHNICAL, AND JUNIOR colleges that participated in the first year of the *Advancing the Humanities* project continue to develop ways to improve the study of the humanities on their campuses. The following pages highlight the humanities accomplishments of eight of these colleges and serve as proof of the continued commitment and dedicated work of all the participants. Programs range from faculty development workshops to the development of core courses to student honors courses; from an examination of ancient Greece and Rome to an exploration of the ideas of the Orient. All are designed to prepare students for personal and professional success in a continually shrinking world. Thus, according to Morrisville College president Frederick Woodward, "*Advancing the Humanities* has stimulated the thought and actions of those participating through an enhanced understanding of multicultural contributions to the humanities."

Amarillo College
Amarillo, Texas

For Amarillo College, participation in the *Advancing the Humanities* project has stimulated development of a new humanities curriculum, a new faculty study program, and a heightened awareness of the purposes of humanities education across the campus. During the first year of participation, the College began two new courses, "Art and Music of the Western World" and "Mythology." In its second year of participation Amarillo College inaugurated a new two-semester course in Western civilization based on texts and films suggested by a volunteer faculty committee. A television version of these courses was also offered through the Amarillo College public television affiliate to meet the needs of students enrolled within a seventy-five-mile radius. Each course includes fifteen hours of television programming and nine two-hour meetings per semester for discussion and testing, as well as weekly writing assignments mailed to the instructor. The second year of participation in the *Advancing the Humanities* project also saw the development of a one-semester course for honors students called "Arts, Ideas, and Civilization."

According to humanities project director Carol Nicklaus, who will be a mentor in the *Developing Regional Humanities Networks* project, "The most dramatic aspect of our participation in the *Advancing the Humanities* project has been the first of two humanities faculty enrichment seminars, made possible by an NEH grant for two such seminars." In the fall of 1990, eighteen faculty members studied Renaissance Florence. Meeting weekly, the group read and discussed some twenty books, articles, and films. Throughout the semester, this faculty group held monthly three-day meetings with Renaissance scholars from University of California at Los Angeles, University of California at Berkeley, Texas A&M University, and Yale University. Some participants received graduate credit through an arrangement with Texas Tech University. Faculty members from across the campus express interest in applying for the 1991 seminar, "Our Sound: American Music and Literature."

In the interest of sharing these humanities offerings with a wider audience, Amarillo College is offering two lecture series this year supported by College funds. The first is a series of four lectures presented by NEH Renaissance scholars at the Amarillo Art Center on the college campus. The second is the continuation of the College's Creative Mind Humanities Lecture Series with the 1991 title "Greek Thought in Contemporary Times." Jointly funded by Amarillo College, Texas Committee for the Humanities, and the Amarillo Association of Yale Alumni, this event utilized an all-Yale University faculty for four lectures in conjunction with the College Theater production of *Medea* and a Greek ceramic exhibit at the Amarillo Art Center. A one-credit evening humanities class has been offered on the same topics as the lectures.

Says Amarillo College president George Miller: "The humanities enhance our quality of life and bring creative beauty and historic and cultural significance into our thinking and being. It is essential that these elements be represented throughout our College curricula. I am proud of the contributions that the *Advancing the Humanities* project, and now our new NEH grant, are making to the quality of life within Amarillo College, its degree and certificate programs, and the Amarillo community at large."

The following is a schedule of the seminars offered to Amarillo College faculty on aspects of the Florentine Renaissance

Renaissance Florence Faculty Enrichment Seminars

Aug. 24	Selections from Petrarch and De Gennaro, Dante's *Divine Comedy*
Aug. 31	Boccaccio, *Decameron*—Introduction; Kallendorf, *In Praise of Aeneas*
Sept. 6–8	Literature scholar: Dr. Craig Kallendorf, Texas A&M University
Sept. 6	Lecture, Amarillo Art Center, "Renaissance Italy and the Birth of the Humanities"
Sept. 14	Burckhardt, *The Civilization of the Renaissance in Italy*; Burke, *The Italian Renaissance*
Sept. 21	Castiglioni, *The Courtier* Biagioli, "Galileo's System of Patronage," "Galileo, the Emblem Maker," "Court Culture and Galileo's Trial"
Sept. 27–29	Science scholar: Dr. Mario Giagioli, UCLA
Sept. 27	Lecture, Amarillo Art Center, "Court Culture and Galileo's Trial," References to *Notebooks of Leonardo da Vinci*
Oct. 5	Hibbert, *The House of Medici* Machiavelli, *The Prince*
Oct. 8–10	History scholar: Dr. Gene Brucker, University of California at Berkeley
Oct. 12	Brucker, *Renaissance Florence* Pico della Mirandola, selections
Oct. 18	Lecture, Amarillo Art Center
Oct. 28	Vasari, *The Lives of the Artists: Vol. I*, selections Film: "The Flowering of Harmony"
Nov. 2	Clark, *Leonardo da Vinci* Baxandall, *Painting and Experience in Fifteenth Century Italy*
Nov. 9	Gilbert, trans., *The Poetry and Letters of Michelangelo* Film: "Return to Glory: Michelangelo Revealed"
Nov. 18–20	Fine arts scholar: Dr. Creighton Gilbert, Yale University
Nov. 19	Lecture Amarillo Art Center, "Michelangelo's Feminism in the Sistine Chapel Ceiling"

Anoka-Ramsey Community College
Coon Rapids, Minnesota

Although for many years Anoka-Ramsey had offered both discipline-specific humanities courses in literature, music, art, philosophy, religion, and history and courses in the study of Western culture through its integrated humanities department, the breadth of the curriculum had failed to provide a clear and unified direction to the student. An outside evaluator characterized the integrated humanities curriculum as rich and challenging, but too skewed to modern world and Western culture offerings and too understaffed with a two-member faculty to address the bias.

Through participation in the *Advancing the Humanities* project, the Anoka-Ramsey team accepted the challenge of working on these problems. Four new part-time humanities instructors were hired to increase integrated offerings to include ancient, medieval, and Renaissance materials as well as to introduce a non-Western integrated humanities course, "Introduction to Africa." The Greco-Roman library collection expanded through major purchases, while videotape purchases of classic dramas, films, and Greek and Roman art history series enriched classroom materials and permitted a restructuring of the ancient and modern world curriculum to include close study of visual and auditory texts in the classroom instruction.

Humanities team members worked to establish humanities-related activities as part of the campus extracurricular life. A student-initiated organization, the Anoka-Ramsey Club for the Humanities, was established to bring students together with faculty to discuss issues vital to the human condition. The club has offered students opportunities to read papers, listen to guest speakers, and take field trips to cultural events and sites. It has also initiated discussions after college theater performances as well as a series of highly successful bag lunch discussions on a range of humanities-oriented issues.

Art and music faculty received a grant from the Minnesota Humanities Commission to fund a series of humanities discussions with accompanying local community library displays on post-modernist art and music. In addition, a series of visiting scholars gave public lectures in connection with an experimental course on global mythology taught in the spring of 1990. Scholars from Finland, England, and this country illustrated how humanities scholarship can help students as well as faculty address issues of common concern across the disciplines. During the 1989–90 academic year, the humanities club and the humanities department faculty helped to add a humanities presence to a campus year-long discussion, "Civilization in Crisis."

Working with their mentors, Gael Tower, Richard Lewis, and Frank Weihs, the Anoka-Ramsey humanities team learned how humanities had been used for faculty renewal at Tacoma Community College, a school with a remarkably similar faculty. Together with Tower, Lewis, and Weihs, the team began to develop a plan through which the humanities could provide a similar opportunity for faculty renewal at Anoka-Ramsey.

With guidance from their mentors, Anoka-Ramsey team members were able to arrange an all-day workshop to introduce the integrated curriculum approach to the campus. The workshop, run by Jean McGregor, Evergreen State College, led to two experiments, one a course in global myth, taught by the integrated humanities instructor along with a philosophy and a sociology instructor, the other an English composition course paired with an introductory sociology course. The approach has already provided significant renewal in the humanities for the College. The *Advancing the Humanities* project created an environment at Anoka-Ramsey Community College in which a dialogue about humanities curriculum has begun, a dialogue which is leading to new consensus about its role in the curriculum.

Butte College
Oroville, California

Although Butte College had offered a number of highly successful humanities courses to its students for several years, there had been no core humanities requirement, and associate degree students had been able to select from among some fifty options to fulfill the single three-unit distribution requirement in the humanities. Through the efforts of its *Advancing the Humanities* team and with the support of its mentors, Karen Bojar and Grace Flisser, Butte began to address this problem.

Team members conducted a faculty-wide survey which resulted in an enthusiastic endorsement of many of the recommendations in the AACJC Humanities Policy Statement. A campus-wide humanities council was formed to discuss various recommendations for strengthening the humanities at Butte College. A seminar on cultural literacy, featuring Bojar and Flisser, was sponsored by the council as part of the College's staff development program.

To move forward toward implementing the recommendations, Butte College applied for and received an NEH planning grant. This grant, which included significant matching support from the College, enabled twelve humanities faculty to collaborate with a like number of their colleagues from various vocational programs as they analyzed texts and ideas relevant to both groups. Using ethics as a unifying theme, the group read and discussed such works as *Lysistrata, Frankenstein, Faust, Death of a Salesman,* and *Brave New World.* In some cases outside scholars were brought in to lead the discussions, while in others, Butte College faculty made presentations. The discussion on *Frankenstein* was co-presented by a faculty member in literature and one in electrical technology.

These discussions were held for a week in the summer and on various Saturdays during the following school year. Common ethical issues were identified and a number of faculty have already indicated specific innovations they intend to introduce in their classes as a result. It is anticipated that a new, team-taught, interdisciplinary core course will be accepted by the humanities council and the curriculum committee as a requirement for all Butte College students and possibly as a prerequisite for all other humanities courses offered by the College. Further funding from NEH will be requested to support the implementation of the new curriculum.

According to Butte's president, Betty Dean, *"Advancing the Humanities* has provided Butte College with the focus and energy necessary not only to strengthen our curriculum, but also to create a stronger collegial bond between the humanities faculty and those who teach in various vocational disciplines. We expect to enjoy the fruits of this labor for many years to come."

Kalamazoo Valley Community College
Kalamazoo, Michigan

Although the humanities program at Kalamazoo Valley Community College had been a generally strong one, faculty and administration at the College agreed that it failed to make adequate connections with the sciences and technology. The *Advancing the Humanities* team focused on ways to link the sciences, technology, and human values through the underlying concept of "connections."

Proof of the team's success has been the awarding of an NEH grant for its project, "The Humanities, Science and Technology: Making Connections." The grant will enable twenty-one members of the faculty, representing the humanities, science, and technology, to sustain a dialogue on the relationship among these disciplines.

Nationally known scholars who are themselves particularly interested in "making connections" will conduct four week-long seminars during two summer institutes to be held in 1991 and 1992. Additional scholars will present colloquia during the academic years that follow the two summer institutes. The faculty members participating in the project will attend the seminars. Furthermore, by January, 1993, a four-credit core course will have been developed and will be taught for the first time. It will focus on how world views from antiquity to modern times shape attitudes toward such diverse subjects as women, the environment, work, and the spirit.

The 1991 summer faculty institute, "Connection Makers Throughout the Centuries," will be led by James Christian, professor of philosophy, Rancho Santiago College, California, who will discuss Plato, Aristotle, and other "connection makers" of antiquity; Tibor Wlassics, professor of Italian, University of Virginia, on Dante; Mary Evelyn Tucker, professor of religion, Bucknell University, on "connection makers" of the Orient; and Wade Robison, professor of philosophy, Kalamazoo, on David Hume. All presentations will underscore the relationship of the humanities with science and technology.

The following summer, the institute will focus on "The City: Where Connections are Made." Speakers and their topics include Harold Morowitz, professor of molecular biophysics and biochemistry, Fairfax University, on "The City: The Spiritual Connection"; Robert Sessions, professor of philosophy, Kirkwood Community College, "The City: The Work Connection"; Judith Zinsser and Bonnie Anderson, co-authors of *A History of Their Own: Women in Europe from Prehistory to the Present,* on "The City: The Gender Connection"; and Robert McGinn, professor of industrial engineering and engineering management, and professor of values, technology, science and society, Stanford University, on "The City: The Ethics Connection."

Under the guidance of mentor Evelyn Edson, the humanities team is, according to project director Robert Badra, "bringing its dream of 'making connections' to life." He adds, "The NEH award will assure that the dream will become a reality."

North Idaho College
Coeur d'Alene, Idaho

When North Idaho College was selected as one of the first-round participants in the *Advancing the Humanities* project, the challenges they faced seemed overwhelming. They had no real humanities program, no group or person in charge of humanities, no shared understanding of what the humanities were, should or could be for their students, no clear voice for the humanities in campus-wide planning or budget decisions, considerable perplexity about how to effectively teach primary works to students with increasingly low basic skills, and a weary veteran faculty in urgent need of personal and professional renewal.

Less than two years later, the humanities at North Idaho College have come a long way. Faculty formed a thirty-four-member humanities network as a permanent campus entity with offical quasi-divisional status but a faculty-led, bottom-up approach to change. It has become the fulcrum of significant campus-wide change and is increasingly drawing colleagues in other disciplines as well as administrators and support staff into its activities, including retreats, formal and informal study, conferences, and speaker series as well as curriculum redesign.

A six-member network steering committee meets weekly and a faculty member with forty percent released time acts as humanities coordinator. Significant steps toward a revitalized humanities program have included intensive reading and discussions with colleagues, students, and community members concerning the humanities' role; developing and widely disseminating a seventy-six-page self-study and long-range plan endorsed by the board of trustees; drafting a group statement based on the Community College Humanities Association guidelines, since adopted by the college curriculum council as criteria for all present and future core humanities courses; a separate budget, earmarked largely for faculty development; substantial humanities representation on the general education committee and curriculum council; and substantive strengthening of humanities teaching by more frequent and effective use of primary works.

A new interdisciplinary humanities core course, "Montage: Introduction to the Humanities," has been designed both for students for
whom this may be an only humanities experience and as a solid
foundation for later single-discipline study in the humanities for Associate in Arts and Associate in Science students. The team-planned
course focuses on critical/creative thinking and communication and is
organized around a five-question inquiry approach, through which
students and faculty explore together highly diverse works in seven to
nine different humanities disciplines or genres in any given semester.

A highlight of the humanities project, and fundamental to attaining
many of its objectives, was a summer seminar in which twenty-two
humanities faculty, a dean, and a librarian spent one week in August,
1990, in intense discussion of a wide variety of works in all humanities
disciplines under the direction of Karl Sandberg, Macalester College,
Minnesota. All seminar participants now qualify to teach the new
course, and most are experimenting with applications of the seminar
in existing courses.

Affirm team members: "The *Advancing the Humanities* project
offered us field-tested models of exciting humanities programs and
institutional renewal efforts; invaluable mentoring by Rhonda Kekke;
and a whole network of supportive and inspiring collegial relationships
with other community colleges around the country. Our recent NEH
grant to fund the network's project, "Meeting of the Minds: Laying
the Groundwork for General Education," will now make it possible
for us to continue this highly satisfying progress, and to share it with
an even wider circle of our colleagues and students." Funded activities
include a month-long interdisciplinary faculty colloquium on "Truth
and Knowing," related study and speaker series throughout the
year, and urgently needed improvement of humanities holdings in the
College's new library. Project director Judith Sylte was chosen to be
a mentor to colleges participating in *Developing Regional Humanities
Networks.*

North Idaho College President C. Robert Bennet observes: "The
humanities project has been the force North Idaho College needed to
bring faculty from the several disciplines together for a common
purpose. Motivated by an excellent summer session with a consultant, instructors are now sharing their talent and ideas. The excitement and energy emanating from this project have a ripple effect that
is having an impact on the entire campus."

Northampton Community College
Bethlehem, Pennsylvania

Northampton Community College has made considerable progress over the past two years in reaching its goal to upgrade the humanities curriculum at the College. The College has developed strategies for dealing with two major problem areas: students who receive associate degrees without taking any humanities courses; and humanities faculty who rarely have the opportunity to teach courses in their fields beyond the introductory or skills level.

As a result of work accomplished through its action plan, the College applied for and was awarded an NEH grant for a set of humanities activities continuing through 1991. The humanities team was able to recruit additional members of the humanities faculty to help plan new courses with general support from other faculty and the administration. In addition, Northampton's college council voted to add a humanities requirement to the general education core for all degree programs as of fall 1992.

A three-semester plan introduced the first two of the College's humanities electives, "The Democratic Experiment, 1776–1900," and "The American Work Experience." In both cases, a faculty group met throughout the first semester for an in-depth study of the tentative course material, under the tutelage of outside scholars. A smaller group continued to meet in "follow-up" sessions the following semester to be well prepared to teach the new course in the third term. "The Democratic Experiment" was taught for the first time in the fall semester of 1990. The two sections of the course examine the intellectual and cultural shaping of America with the support of primary sources and field trips. "The American Work Experience," an inter-disciplinary course designed to reach out to College business and technology programs, was scheduled for Spring 1991.

Northampton Community College received valuable support from its mentors: team members reported that "Gael Tower was especially willing to 'beat the drum' for our action plan among our faculty and the administration and he encouraged us to speak directly to all persons whose cooperation would be key to the plan's success."

The team was also gratified by the support it received from administrators and other faculty on the Northampton campus. Three business faculty members agreed to participate in a colloquium on the American workplace. An assistant dean has been part of the planning team from the start, and the vice president spent a full day on mentor Gael Tower's campus, Tacoma Community College. Final proof of the success of the project is in the choice of Northampton Community College as a mentor college for AACJC's new *Developing Regional Humanities Networks* project.

Saddleback College
Mission Viejo, California

Through its participation in the *Advancing the Humanities* project, Saddleback College continues to seek ways to expand its humanities course content beyond Western culture, to make the program more coherent, and to strengthen the humanities across the curriculum.

As a result of a series of first-year initiatives including interdisciplinary colloquia, in-service retreats, and a faculty development program devoted to a study of Chinese and Japanese literature, the College has continued to expand in many directions across the curriculum, across cultures, and into the community. Motivated by the faculty retreats, instructors of two one-year humanities courses explore the Renaissance primarily in Italy for the first semester and Islamic cultures, China, and Japan, as well as subcultures of America for the second semester.

A monthly humanities hour regularly features speakers on multicultural themes. A recent program on the historical and political background of the Persian Gulf crisis drew hundreds and was televised throughout the community.

In spring 1990, the Saddleback College Regional Center of the California Humanities Project acted as host to a successful mini-institute for junior and senior high school teachers on the Renaissance. The Center also "adopted" a local elementary school with a predominant minority population in a humanities partnership.

The following fall, the humanities team gave a presentation at the annual CCHA conference to disseminate the objectives and results of its project. The humanities team will act as host for the fall 1991 CCHA conference.

Finally, the College is re-evaluating its multi-section Western culture survey course to consider possible formats for a humanities core course and for the inclusion of multicultural texts.

Members of the Saddleback *Advancing the Humanities* team are quick to praise their mentor for her support: "Agnes Pollock has been enormously helpful in showing how to overcome the inherent insularity of our academic departments. Our faculty now realize that we are in an excellent position to be the center for humanistic study in our community."

Adds President Constance Carroll: "The Saddleback plan for faculty development represents the culmination of a series of important steps exploring new areas of the humanities and expanding interdisciplinary collaboration at Saddleback College, thanks to the groundwork laid in the *Advancing the Humanities* project. This project has my full support and unqualified recommendation for funding, as an important vehicle for substantive intellectual inquiry and vibrant debate, leading to the College's full emergence as a community center for the humanities."

Recently, Saddleback College was awarded an NEH grant for its project, "Building Bridges: Faculty Development in the Humanities Through Faculty Study Institutes." With the aid of the grant, and following on the heels of its successful study of Chinese and Japanese literature, the College team arranged for a second study institute, this time focusing on the literature of Latin America.

Snow College
Ephraim, Utah

Motivated by their participation in the *Advancing the Humanities* project, Snow College humanities team members have continued to work actively to change the humanities program at the College and to make these changes on a far more rational and informed basis. They are maintaining their goal of presenting students with a coherent view of the role of the humanities and demonstrating to them that the humanities form a distinctive discipline with a world view that is both articulate and meaningful.

When the College decided on an overall revision of its general education program, humanities team members designed an interdisciplinary humanities course which was approved by the curriculum committee. The new required five-hour course, taking the place of an introduction to literature course, retains a significant literature component, but integrates the component with approaches to art, music, philosophy, and history. The class sets the stage for two subsequent humanities required classes, one a theory and one a practice class. "We really want the study of the humanities to become 'hands on' experience—not merely a theoretical appreciation," explains humanities team member Susan Burdett. For example, a student not majoring in art would take the introduction to the humanities course followed by a survey of art and watercolors.

Snow College faculty and administrators are hopeful that the institution of such a program for all degree-seeking students will ensure that they have a common experience to draw upon in subsequent courses and throughout their education. It will enable them to recognize that the humanities offer a vision of the world that is both valuable and unique through exposure to the works of great writers and thinkers.

Participation in the *Advancing the Humanities* project, including site visits with mentor Lorain Stowe, has resulted in a faculty much more open to the idea of a core humanities course. Administrators are most supportive, evidenced by a recent statement by Snow College President Gerald Day: "The AACJC/NEH *Advancing the Humanities* project has been helpful in three ways: it has provided a forum for and exchange of ideas about the role the humanities play in the College curriculum; it has encouraged program innovation; and it has improved the morale of the faculty. These benefits are timely because the humanities division will be moving into its new building* as soon as renovations are completed. Our students will be engaged in a revitalized humanities program that has the support of the faculty and administration of Snow College."

*Snow College has received an NEH Challenge Grant to help fund a new humanities building.

Below is a brief description of Snow College's new interdiscipliary humanities course

Humanities 201—Credit: 3 quarter hours

Humanities 201 is an interdisciplinary introduction to the humanities. Its purpose is to introduce the student to the ways we human beings have expressed our response to existence and our search for meaning. The class provides background to the humanities, introduces important terminology, and encourages curiosity and questioning in the students. It will be conducted in a lecture/discussion format.

Textbooks

Required: *Arts, Ideas, and Civilization* by Hobbs, or *The Art of Being Human* by Janaro

Primary works (final selections chosen at the discretion of instructors):

The *Iliad,* Homer

Oedipus Rex, Sophocles

Apology, Plato

The New Testament

The Inferno, from *Divine Comedy,* Dante

Hamlet, William Shakespeare

The Misanthrope, Jean Baptiste Moliere

Reveries of a Solitary Walker, Jean-Jacques Rousseau

Dubliners, James Joyce

Assignments: Students will be required to write a mimimum of 3000 words to complete the course. Students will be assigned three themes. There will be a midterm and a final two-hour examination.

Part VII
DEVELOPING REGIONAL HUMANITIES NETWORKS: A NEW INITIATIVE

IN ITS CONTINUING QUEST FOR WAYS TO IMPROVE THE study of the humanities at the nation's community, technical, and junior colleges, the American Association of Community and Junior Colleges, in cooperation with the Community College Humanities Association (CCHA), has launched a new two-year project entitled *Developing Regional Humanities Networks*. The project is supported by the National Endowment for the Humanities in the amount of $367,795, representing eighty percent of total project costs.

Building upon the two years of community college humanities improvement activities already designed and implemented through the NEH-funded *Advancing the Humanities* project, the primary purpose of the new AACJC initiative is to establish regional humanities networks in each CCHA region. Through these networks, humanities faculty will be able to benefit from colleagues' experience and expertise in humanities programming. These regional humanities networks will be established during the coming two years, but will continue beyond the project period.

The project will showcase exemplary community college humanities programs at regional conferences held in each of the five CCHA regions: Eastern (Connecticut, Delaware, Maine, Maryland, Massachusetts, New Hampshire, New Jersey, New York, Pennsylvania, Puerto Rico, Rhode Island, Vermont, Washington D.C.); Pacific-Western (Alaska, California, Hawaii, Idaho, Montana, Nevada, Ore-

Landon Kirchner, second from left, leads mentor training session at the Southern Regional Humanities Conference, Atlanta, February 8, 1991.

gon, Washington, Wyoming); Southern (Alabama, Florida, Georgia, Kentucky, Mississippi, North Carolina, South Carolina, Tennessee, Virginia, West Virginia); Central (Illinois, Indiana, Iowa, Michigan, Minnesota, Missouri, Nebraska, North Dakota, Ohio, South Dakota, Wisconsin); and Southwestern (Arizona, Arkansas, Colorado, Kansas, Louisiana, New Mexico, Oklahoma, Texas, Utah). Fifty colleges are being selected to attend the regional conferences, receive the services of a mentor, and participate in the development of networking activities.

The project is designed to be most helpful to those institutions that have identified specific needs in their humanities programs and have begun to think about ways to address these needs. Three major sets of activities are in progress.

In each region, the project begins with a two-day working conference at which a two-member humanities faculty team from each college, with help from a mentor, designs an action plan of activities to be implemented over the coming year to improve humanities programs at the college. A third team member, an administrator, is encouraged to attend, as well. In addition to participating in the intensive team/mentor meetings at which their individual projects' action plans are formulated, college teams learn about successful humanities programs that effectively engage students and faculty with humanities works of enduring value. NEH staff members are available to describe possible funding opportunities.

In 1992, one year after the first conference, team members will reunite at a second weekend regional conference to share progress on their new humanities initiatives and work with AACJC staff and CCHA leaders to establish regional humanities networks.

Second, *Developing Regional Humanities Networks* participants continue to work with their mentors during the period between the regional conferences via telephone and mail, as well as in person. Each college receives a site visit from its mentor. A full-day pre-planned agenda for the site visit includes time to meet with the project team as well as the opportunity for the mentor to meet with college administrators and humanities faculty to discuss the college's humanities program. Following the visit, the college team submits a site visit report to AACJC documenting how the visit helped advance the team's humanities action plan.

Third, *ADVANCING THE HUMANITIES NEWS* is being published throughout the project. The newsletter presents brief case studies on the exemplary programs and progress reports on activities at the selected colleges. It also features articles on the humanities and other items of interest to humanities faculty and administrators.

Exemplary projects for *Developing Regional Humanities Networks* cover a broad range of activities and strategies for bringing the study of the humanities to the students and faculties of the nation's community colleges. Directors of these projects will serve as mentors to the selected colleges as they develop faculty study programs that focus on one figure, such as Shakespeare or Dante, one topic, such as mythology or ethics, or a range of topics leading to curriculum development. Curriculum development projects themselves may focus on developing core courses in the humanities, revitalizing introductory humanities courses, developing new humanities programs to engage career and occupational students or to challenge honors students, or strengthening foreign language programs. Thus, each selected college has the opportunity to learn from an institutional model that best suits its own specific academic needs.

AACJC's *Developing Regional Humanities Networks* project is being directed by James F. Gollattscheck, AACJC executive vice president, managed by Diane U. Eisenberg, and coordinated by Diana H. Metcalf. The project's goal is to ensure that participating humanities faculty and administrators benefit from the knowledge and experience of their colleagues, share their expertise in humanities programming, and establish formal avenues or "networks" for revitalization that will endure well beyond the project period.

Developing Regional Humanities Networks—Selected Colleges*

EASTERN REGION:

Bristol Community College, MA
Bucks County Community College, PA
Community College of Vermont
County College of Morris, NJ
Frederick Community College, MD
Harrisburg Area Community College, PA
Housatonic Community College, CT
Manor Junior College, PA
Mohawk Valley Community College, NY
Southern Maine Technical College, ME

PACIFIC-WESTERN REGION:

Central Oregon Community College, OR
Central Wyoming College, WY
Cerritos College, CA
Chaffey Community College, CA
North Seattle Community College, WA
Olympic College, WA
Pasadena City College, CA
Solano Community College, CA
Spokane Community College, WA
Windward Community College, HI

SOUTHERN REGION:

Catawba Valley Community College, NC
Danville Community College, VA
Dyersburg State Community College, TN
Manatee Community College, FL
Nashville State Technical Institute, TN
New River Community College, VA
Orangeburg-Calhoun Technical College, SC
Pellissippi State Technical Community College, TN
Seminole Community College, FL
Technical College of the Lowcountry, SC

At this report's publication date, thirty colleges had been selected; an additional twenty colleges remained to be selected in the coming months.

Part VIII
APPENDICES

APPENDICES

Advancing the Humanities Participants

MENTORS

Community College of Philadelphia
1700 Spring Garden Street
Philadelphia, PA 19130
(215) 751-8331

Karen Bojar, English Department
Grace Flisser, English Department

Edmonds Community College
20000 68th Avenue West
Lynnwood, WA 98036-5999
(206) 771-1500

Barbara Morgridge, English Department

Jefferson State Community College
2601 Carson Road
Birmingham, AL 35215-3098
(205) 853-1200

Agnes Pollock, English Department

Kirkwood Community College
6301 Kirkwood Boulevard West
Cedar Rapids, IA 52406
(319) 398-5537

Joseph Collins, Electronics Department
Rhonda Kekke, Communication Arts Department
Robert Sessions, Communication Arts Department

Middlesex County College
155 Mill Road
Edison, NJ 08818
(201) 548-6000

Kathy Fedorko, English Department

Nassau Community College
Garden City, NY 11530-6793
(516) 222-7177

Bernice W. Kliman, English Department

Piedmont Virginia Community College
Route 6 Box 1A
Charlottesville, VA 22901
(804) 977-3900

Evelyn Edson, History Department

Prince George's Community College
301 Largo Road
Largo, MD 20772-2199
(301) 322-0414

Isa Engleberg, Faculty and Academic Services

Richland College
12800 Abrams Road
Dallas, TX 75243-2199
(214) 238-6200

Lee Paez, Honors Program, Classics Program

Utah Valley Community College
800 West 1200 South
Orem, UT 84058
(801) 222-8000

Elaine Englehardt, Humanities Department

PARTICIPATING COLLEGES

Adirondack Community College
28 Broadacres Road
Glens Falls, NY 12804

Charles Gotsch, Academic Dean (518) 793-4491
Paul Muscari, Chair, Humanities Division (518) 793-6535
Jean Rikhoff, Chair, English Division (518) 793-4491

Allen County Community College
1801 North Cottonwood
Iola, KS 66749

Van Thompson, Instructor, History (316) 365-5116

Berkshire Community College
1350 West Street
Pittsfield, MA 01201

Mario Caluori, Professor, English (413) 499-4660
Emily Jahn, Chair, English Department (413) 499-4660
Sandra Kurtinitis, Academic Dean (413) 499-4660, ext. 277
Faith Vosburgh, Chair, Humanities Division (413) 499-4660, ext. 328

Blue Ridge Community College
P.O. Box 80
Weyers Cave, VA 24486

Darrell Hurst, Professor, English (703) 234-9261
Robert Jobin, Instructor, English, Philosophy, and German (703) 234-9261
Metro Lazorack, Dean of Instruction and Student Services (703) 234-9261,
    ext. 207

Cabrillo College
6500 Soquel Drive
Aptos, CA 95003

Nancy Brown, Instructor, Philosophy (408) 479-6401
Joseph McNeilly, Instructor, English (408) 479-6100
Ann Stephenson, Vice President for Instruction (408) 479-6451
Peter Varcados, Instructor, History (408) 479-0369

Central Florida Community College
P.O. Box 1388
Ocala, FL 32678-1388

Patricia Heinicke, Instructor, Humanities and Social Sciences (904) 237-2111,
    ext. 631
Ira Holmes, Chair, Humanities and Social Sciences (904) 237-2111, ext. 293
Kevin Mulholland, Instructor, Humanities and Social Sciences (904) 237-2111,
    ext. 297
Scott Olsen, Associate Professor, Humanities and Social Sciences
    (904) 237-2111. ext. 236

Chemeketa Community College
4000 Lancaster Drive NE
P.O. Box 14007
Salem, OR 97309-7070

Ed Cochrane, Instructor, History (503) 399-2531
Leonard Held, Instructor, Writing, Film, and Literature (503) 399-2531
Bernard Knab, Director, Humanities and Communications (503) 399-2531

Clark State Community College
570 East Leffel Lane
Springfield, OH 45501

Judith Anderson, Associate Professor, English (513) 328-6030
Marsha Bordner, Chair, Arts and Sciences (513) 325-0691
Charles Dickson, Assistant Professor, Western Civilization and Geography
(513) 328-6030

Community College of Allegheny County—South Campus
1750 Clairton Road
West Mifflin, PA 15122

Betsy Adams, Associate Professor, Communication Arts (412) 469-1100
Mary Frances Archey, Assistant Dean for Liberal and Fine Arts
(412) 469-6304
Virginia Hadley, Professor, Communication Arts (412) 469-1100

Eastern Wyoming College
3200 West C Street
Torrington, WY 82240

Daniel Doherty, Chair, Humanities and Fine Arts (307) 532-7111
Sue Ellen Milner, Instructor, Art and Humanities (307) 532-7111
John Nesbitt, Instructor, Spanish, English, and Literature (307) 532-7111

Elgin Community College
1700 Spartan Drive
Elgin, IL 60123

Walter Garrett, Instructor, Humanities (708) 888-7379
Polly Nash-Wright, Dean, Liberal Arts and General Education (708) 888-7379
Suzanne Peterson, Instructor, Art History (708) 888-7379

Genesee Community College
One College Road
Batavia, NY 14020-9704

RayLene Corgiat, Associate Dean, Curriculum and Instruction (716) 343-0055
Margaret Williams, Professor, English (716) 343-0055, ext. 278
Donna Wojcik, Instructor, Business (716) 343-0055

Hawaii Community College
Hilo, HI 96720-4091

Barry Guerrero, Instructor, English (808) 933-3623
Trina Nahm-Mijo, Chair, General Education (808) 933-3422
Kayleen Sato, Instructor, English (808) 933-3537

Iowa Central Community College
330 Avenue "M"
Fort Dodge, IA 50501

Bette Conkin, Instructor, Language Arts (515) 576-7201
Mary Sula Linney, Department Head, Language Arts/Humanities
(515) 576-7201
Roger Natte, Instructor, Social Sciences (515) 576-7201

Lake City Community College
Route 3, Box 7
Lake City, FL 32055

Charles Carroll, Instructor, Humanities (904) 752-1822
Tim Moses, Instructor, Humanities (904) 752-1822
David Richards, Dean of Instructional Support (904) 752-1822

Lake Michigan College
2755 East Napier Avenue
Benton Harbor, MI 49022-1899

William Sprunk, Professor, English (616) 927-3571, ext. 212
K. Sundaram, Professor, Philosophy; Director, Honors Program
(616) 927-3571, ext. 336
Michael Walsh, Dean, Liberal Arts and General Studies (616) 927-3571,
ext. 214

Massachusetts Bay Community College
50 Oakland Street
Wellesley Hills, MA 02181

Marie Callahan, Associate Dean for Liberal Arts (617) 237-1100, ext. 581
Eleanor Smith, Assistant Professor, Business (617) 237-1100
Harold White, Professor, Humanities (617) 237-1100
Walter Zuschlag, Automative Service Training Administrator (508) 478-4475

Middlesex Community College
Springs Road
Bedford, MA 01730

Sandra Albertson-Shea, Associate Professor, English (617) 275-8910
Julien Farland, Professor, Philosophy (617) 275-8910
Kent Mitchell, Chair, Humanities Division (617) 275-8910, ext. 4411

Mississippi Gulf Coast Community College
17317 Woodrow Wilson Drive
Gulfport, MS 39503

Joan Fitch, Director, Honors Program (601) 896-3355, ext. 215
James "Pat" Smith, Instructor, History and Psychology (601) 896-3355
William Therrell, Instructor, History (601) 896-3355

Northeast Texas Community College
P.O. Box 1307
Mt. Pleasant, TX 75455

Ron Clinton, Coordinator, Fine Arts and Humanities; Director, Music
(214) 572-1911
Susan McBride, Dean of Instruction (214) 572-1911
Benton White, Director, Social Sciences; Instructor, History (214) 572-1911

Northern Virginia Community College—Loudoun Campus
Loudon Campus-NVCC
Sterling, VA 22170

Beverly Blois, Professor, History (703) 450-2527
R. Neil Reynolds, Provost (703) 450-2517
Agatha Taormina, Professor, English (703) 450-2528
David Whipple, Assistant Professor, Art History (703) 450-2527

Pennsylvania College of Technology
One College Avenue
Williamsport, PA 17701

Daniel Doyle, Professor, History and Philosophy (717) 326-3761
Veronica Muzic, Professor, English (717) 326-3761, ext. 7404
Ernest Zebrowski, Jr., Director, Integrated Studies (717) 326-3761

Salt Lake Community College
P.O. Box 30808
Salt Lake City, UT 84130

Pamela Gardner, Chair, Humanities (801) 967-4093
Patricia Hadley, Coordinator, English and Humanities (801) 967-4192
Judith Lunt, Associate Professor, English and Humanities (801) 967-4338

South Puget Sound Community College
2011 Mottman Road SW
Olympia, WA 98502

Michael Beehler, Dean of Instruction (206) 754-7711
Theresa Crater, Instructor, English (206) 754-7711
Phyllis Villeneuve, Instructor, English (206) 754-7711

Thomas Nelson Community College
P.O. Box 9407
Hampton, VA 23670

Eirlys Barker, Assistant Professor, History (804) 825-2792
John Dever, Acting Chair, Communications and Humanities (804) 825-2799
Gerald Safko, Associate Professor, English (804) 825-2946

PROJECT PRINCIPALS

William Askins
Executive Director, Community College Humanities Association
and Professor of English
Community College of Philadelphia
1700 Spring Garden Street
Philadelphia, PA 19130
(215) 751-8860

Selection Committee Member

Diane U. Eisenberg
President, Eisenberg Associates
444 North Capitol Street, Suite 406
Washington, DC 20001
(202) 393-2208

Project Manager

James F. Gollattscheck
Executive Vice President
American Association of Community and Junior Colleges
One Dupont Circle, NW, Suite 410
Washington, DC 20036
(202) 728-0200

Project Director

Judith Jeffrey Howard
Coordinator for Community Colleges
National Endowment for the Humanities
1100 Pennsylvania Avenue, NW, Room 302
Washington, DC 20506
(202) 786-0380

NEH Program Officer

Landon C. Kirchner
Assistant Dean, Arts, Humanities and Social Sciences
Johnson County Community College
12345 College at Quivira
Overland Park, KS 66210
(913) 469-3856

Project Evaluator

Anne S. McNutt
President
Technical College of the Lowcountry
100 South Ribaut Road
Beaufort, SC 29902-1288
(803) 525-8247

Selection Committee Member

Diana H. Metcalf
Staff Member
American Association of Community and Junior Colleges
One Dupont Circle, NW, Suite 410
Washington, DC 20036
(202) 728-0200

Project Coordinator

Jerry Sue Owens
President
Lakewood Community College
3401 Century Avenue
White Bear Lake, MN 55110
(612) 779-3200

Selection Committee Member

Barbara C. Shapiro
Editorial Services
3805 Gramercy Street, NW
Washington, DC 20016
(202) 966-2265

Writer/Editor

George B. Vaughan
Director, Center for Community College Education
George Mason University
4400 University Drive
Fairfax, VA 22030-4444
(703) 764-6484

Selection Committee Member

Nationwide Participation in the
Advancing The Humanities: Year Two Project

- ■ Twelve mentor colleges
- ● Twenty-five colleges selected to participate in Year Two, serving over 140,000 students
- ▲ Twenty-four colleges selected to participate in Year One, serving almost 200,000 students

AACJC HUMANITIES POLICY STATEMENT
The Study of the Humanities in Community, Technical, and Junior Colleges

I. What Do We Mean by the Humanities?

THE HUMANITIES ARE WAYS OF THINKING ABOUT WHAT IS human—about our diverse histories, imaginations, values, words, and dreams. The humanities analyze, interpret, and refine our experience, its comedies and tragedies, struggles, and achievements. They embrace history and art history, literature and film, philosophy and morality, comparative religion, jurisprudence, political theory, languages and linguistics, anthropology, and some of the inquiries of the social sciences. When we ask who we are, and what our lives ought to mean, we are using the humanities.

In addition to the specific content of this roster of disciplines, the humanities represent an approach to learning—an approach which is characterized by certain beliefs about the value of what is worthy of our interest and study. The study of the humanities ranges from the reading of great texts to the understanding of the contemporary, yet perennial, concerns of the human family. The methods of the humanities encompass the methods of the particular disciplines as well as the methods of broader, interdisciplinary inquiry such as the critical and imaginative use of language, texts, and other artifacts of human experience. Whether in content or method, however, study

This statement was adopted and approved by the AACJC Board of Directors on April 12, 1986.

in the humanities always has as its fundamental objective to reveal that which is significant about human life—past, present, and to the extent possible, the future.

II. Why Study the Humanities at Community Colleges?

Learning in the humanities is particularly critical in community, technical, and junior colleges because of the strong interest on the part of students in practical education. It is important that students become economically self-supporting. But it is equally important for them to broaden their horizons so they may participate willingly and wisely in a fuller range of human activity.

The humanities do have inherent worth. The proper study of the humanities, however, is also decidedly practical. For example, the development of advanced technologies requires not only higher-order processes of intelligence, but also a keen appreciation of the impact of technology on the human environment. The humanities concentrate in direct ways on skills of the mind and skills of language, while the ability to reason clearly and communicate well should be a goal of all branches of study. These capabilities, by their very nature, are especially connected to the humanities. The medium of the humanities is essentially language, and their use of language sets in motion reflection and judgment. The humanities assist in developing insights and capacities that are essential for a well-formed public life as well as a fulfilling private one.

The concerns of the humanities extend to many enduring and fundamental questions which confront all human beings in the course of their lives: What is justice? What is courage? What should be loved? What deserves to be defended? What is noble? What is base?

Community college faculty must teach the humanities to their students so that each student is better able to discover a sense of relationships among life, work, and circumstances; to understand self and society through different eyes, places, and times; to reflect on the way personal origins and beliefs affect actions and values; to encounter questions and answers posed in the past; and to raise similar questions about the present and future.

Study of the humanities nurtures the imagination and offers individual and private pleasure. Study of the humanities encourages the best habits of mind. Study of the humanities fosters disciplined approaches to questions that do not have necessarily correct answers. Study of the humanities promotes an enhanced ability to make value judgments—to select the wiser course of action. Study of the humanities inculcates a sense of common culture, encouraging civic purpose and citizenship practices. Study of the humanities seeks balance between the individual and society while fostering the basis of any civilized society—civility and mutuality.

Beyond responsibility to their students, community colleges have a further obligation to the communities they serve. It follows that they should teach the humanities to *all* students so that social cohesion may be fostered through shared understanding, language, and values. Community college students should study the humanities for a seemingly simple reason—to gain knowledge and ability to think concretely about important social and personal questions and to communicate these thoughts through clear and effective written expression. The practical demands of life—both private and public—are illuminated and made more valuable by the study of the humanities.

III. Recommendations to Community College Leaders

The ferment in higher education, reflected by the many calls for educational reform from all quarters, suggests that now is an opportune time for educational leaders to speak out on behalf of the importance of the humanities to the associate degree offered by community colleges. To that end, the following recommendations are offered:

Recommendation 1. Educational policy concerning the humanities and their place in the community college curriculum should be framed within the context of an overall policy on a liberal or general education program of study.

Recommendation 2. Study in the humanities should be a required part of every degree program offered by community colleges.

Recommendation 3. Study in the humanities disciplines should be required beyond existing college requirements for such courses as composition, public speaking, and communications.

In order to assure that the humanities maintain their proper place in the curriculum, it is crucial that the following degree requirements be made public and manifest via the endorsement of the highest policy and administrative bodies—trustees, presidents, academic deans, and other administrators. Hence:

Recommendation 4. A minimum of six semester hours in the humanities for the degree of associate in applied science.

Recommendation 5. A minimum of nine semester hours in the humanities for the degree of associate in science.

Recommendation 6. A minimum of twelve semester hours in the humanities for the degree of associate in arts.

The manner of teaching college courses, as well as the content of courses, especially courses with specific humanities content, is vital to the educational process. Instruction in the humanities must engage students extensively in activities that take them beyond the mere acquisition of facts and the comprehension of principles and theories. Students must be asked to understand the human circumstances that the materials address and to consider critically alternative points of view. Therefore:

Recommendation 7. Humanities courses should develop students' abilities to participate in reflective discourse, to question, analyze, and understand. To develop these abilities, humanities classes must include extensive reading, writing, speaking, and critical analysis of the perspectives, cultures, and traditions that make up our intellectual heritage.

Community colleges serve a wide and varied population, with the typical student body reflecting diversity in age, sex, ethnicity, and interests. The faculty of these institutions, being most familiar with student needs, should take the lead in building appropriate humanities programs. Therefore:

Recommendation 8. The faculty within each institution should develop a comprehensive plan for helping their students achieve knowledge of and sophistication in the humanities. This plan should include a coherent program of courses in sequence, with clear indication of which courses in the humanities are basic, which courses presuppose others, which courses are best taken concurrently with others, and which courses constitute appropriate selection for students who will take limited coursework in the humanities.

It is important that good teaching be the basis for faculty promotion and recognition. To encourage and assist good teachers to continue in the profession and to stimulate others to develop good teaching skills, three recommendations are offered:

Recommendation 9. Evidence of good teaching should be used as an explicit criterion for hiring, promotion, tenure, and other forms of professional recognition. This will demand the development of appropriate measures of teaching ability and effectiveness.

Recommendation 10. Faculty development resources should be used to help faculty develop their teaching skills and further their knowledge of their discipline. Fulltime faculty, and in every instance possible, parttime faculty as well, should be encouraged to attend the meetings and conferences and read the publications of those academic organizations which are increasingly turning their attention to the quality of teaching in our colleges.

Recommendation 11. Funds should be made available to college libraries and learning resource centers for the purchase of materials that support research, provide the basis for cultural enrichment, and constitute resources for programs in the humanities.

Humanities studies do not, and should not, end in high school. Neither should they begin and end in college. Courses of humanistic study can and should be integrated so that high schools and colleges can build on the habits of mind and knowledge acquired by students in their early classes and developed in later ones. Therefore, it is recommended that articulation processes be developed to meet these goals:

Recommendation 12. Governing boards, administrators, and faculties of community colleges, high schools, and four-year colleges should work together to plan a unified and coherent humanities curriculum for their students.

It is urgent that these recommendations be circulated widely to college administrators, legislative officials, and college faculty, as well as to the public and private presses. The recommendations are addressed to community college leaders—presidents, governing boards, administrators, faculty, and curriculum committees. Responsibility for placing the importance of humanities study before the college community and mobilizing activites in its support belongs to each community college president.

ABOUT THE AUTHORS

Diane U. Eisenberg, AACJC senior consultant and manager of the *Advancing the Humanities* project, is president, Eisenberg Associates, a Washington, DC-based educational consulting firm. A former NEH staff member, she has designed, directed, and advised on the development of humanities programs for AACJC and other national organizations. She has served on the Board of Directors of the Community College Humanities Association, co-edited *The Future of Humanities Education in Community, Technical, and Junior Colleges,* and co-authored *Improving Humanities Studies at Community, Technical, and Junior Colleges.*

James F. Gollattscheck, AACJC executive vice president and director of the *Advancing the Humanities* project, has served on the Board of Directors of the Florida Endowment for the Humanities and as a member of the advisory committees for AACJC's previous national humanities projects. He is the founder of COMBASE, a coalition of two-year colleges which stress community-based education, and former president of the Coalition of Adult Education Organizations. Dr. Gollattscheck directed the AACJC/NEH Humanities Roundtable project and co-edited the resulting publication, *The Future of Humanities Education in Community, Technical, and Junior Colleges.* In addition, he co-authored *Improving Humanities Studies at Community, Technical, and Junior Colleges.*

Diana H. Metcalf, AACJC staff member for the *Advancing the Humanities* project and associate editor of ADVANCING THE HUMANITIES NEWS, is an experienced grants administrator. She has coordinated activities for over twenty-five federal grants at the University of California-Davis, the University of Illinois-Urbana, and the University of Wisconsin-Madison. She co-authored *Improving Humanities Studies at Community, Technical, and Junior Colleges.*

117

Barbara C. Shapiro, English teacher and past department chair, Madeira School, McLean, Virginia, is a Washington, DC-based freelance writer/editor. Dr. Shapiro has edited publications for The Community College Press and co-authored *Improving Humanities Studies at Community, Technical, and Junior Colleges.* She has served on the Assessment Policy Committee of the National Assessment of Educational Progress.

ABOUT AACJC

Founded in 1920, with headquarters in Washington, D.C., the American Association of Community and Junior Colleges (AACJC) represents the interests of the 1,211 public and private community, technical, and junior colleges in service to the nation. Mobilizing the considerable strengths and resources of this entire community college network, the Association endeavors to help these colleges continue to meet the challenges of a rapidly changing environment and provide our citizens with economically feasible opportunities for educational excellence.

- AACJC's publications program provides the latest news, scholarly thinking, and research for education professionals. Publications include the bimonthly *Community, Technical, and Junior College Journal;* the *Community, Technical, and Junior College Times,* AACJC's biweekly newspaper; and the *AACJC Letter,* a monthly newsletter from AACJC's president to presidents and chancellors of AACJC member institutions.

   Of special interest to readers of this publication is *Improving Humanities Studies at Community, Technical, and Junior Colleges,* a progress report on the first year of the *Advancing the Humanities* project. Copies of this publication are available for $11.00 each ($8.75 for AACJC members) from AACJC Publication Sales, 2700 Prosperity Avenue, Fairfax, VA 22031, telephone (703) 204-0411, FAX (703) 207-9862.

- The Community College Press publishes hardcover books, including the following recent publications: *Dateline 2000: The New Higher Education Agenda* by Dale Parnell; *Underrepresentation and the Question of Diversity: Women and Minorities in Community Colleges* by Rosemary Gillett-Karam, Suanne

Roueche, and John Roueche; and *Profiles in Success: Reflections on the Community College Experience* by Robert Bahruth and Phillip Venditti, Eds. These can be ordered from AACJC at the above address.

ABOUT NEH

The National Endowment for the Humanities (NEH) was established by an act of Congress in 1963. It is an independent grant-making agency of the federal government that supports research, education, and public programs in the humanities. Grants are made through five divisions: Education Programs, Fellowships and Seminars, General Programs, Research Programs, and State Programs. In addition, they are made through the Office of Challenge Grants and the Office of Preservation.

In the act that established the National Endowment for the Humanities, the term *humanities* includes, but is not limited to, the study of the following disciplines: history; philosophy; languages; linguistics; literature; archaeology; jurisprudence; the history, theory, and criticism of the arts; ethics; comparative religion; and those aspects of the social sciences that employ historical or philosophical approaches.

The National Endowment for the Humanities supports exemplary work to advance and disseminate knowledge in all the disciplines of the humanities. Endowment support is intended to complement and assist private and local efforts and to serve as a catalyst to increase nonfederal support for projects of high quality.

Although the activities funded by the Endowment vary greatly in cost, in the numbers of people involved, and in their specific intents and benefits, they all have in common two requirements for funding: significance to learning in the humanities, and excellence in conception. In the most general terms, NEH-supported projects aid scholarship and research in the humanities, help improve humanities education, and foster in the American people a greater curiosity about and understanding of the humanities.

ABOUT CCHA

The Community College Humanities Association (CCHA) is a national, non-profit organization devoted to strengthening the humanities in the nation's public and private community, technical, and junior colleges. The only national organization of its kind for humanities faculty in two-year colleges, CCHA also serves as a Council of the American Association of Community and Junior Colleges. CCHA has the following purposes:

- to advance the cause of the humanities through its own activities and in cooperation with other institutions and groups involved in higher education;
- to provide a regular forum for the exchange of ideas on significant issues in the humanities and in higher education;
- to encourage and support the professional work of faculty in the humanities;
- to sponsor conferences and institutes which provide opportunities for faculty development and enrichment;
- to promote the discussion of issues of concern to faculty and administrators in the humanities;
- to disseminate information through the publications of the Association.

CCHA is organized into five regional divisions and acts as host to five regional conferences which alternate yearly with national conferences. In addition, it administers a national awards program, a literary magazine competition, a mini-grant program, and special initiatives in the humanities. CCHA publishes a tri-annual newletter, *The Community College Humanist,* and a scholarly journal, *The Community College Humanities Review.*